*W*RITING

WRITING A NOVEL

Rosemary Aitken

The Crowood Press

First published in 2003 by
The Crowood Press Ltd
Ramsbury, Marlborough
Wiltshire SN8 2HR

www.crowood.com

British Library Cataloguing-in-Publication Data
A catalogue record for this book is available from the British Library.

ISBN 1 86126 608 1

Typeset by Jean Cussons Typesetting, Diss, Norfolk

Printed and bound in Great Britain by The Bath Press

CONTENTS

Dedication

To Julia.

1   GETTING STARTED

KNOWING YOUR OWN STRENGTHS

Writing a novel is an exciting goal! Of course, it is not easy. It will require dedication to write and revise thousands of words, but if you have the determination to tackle this you already have one of the most important ingredients for success. Of course, there can be no guarantee, and the road to publication can be a long and rocky one, but if you are prepared to work and approach your task with curiosity and an open mind you already have a head-start along that road – and you have demonstrated some of those qualities simply by picking up this book.

There are other important requisites too which you almost certainly possess, although you may not be wholly aware of them nor of their value in writing successfully. The first is your precious individuality. You are an individual, with your own individual imagination, knowledge, experience and enthusiasms. This combination is unique to you and will be the basis for everything you write, whether your novel is set in present-day suburbia or on an imaginary planet thousands of years in the future; in the world of international espionage or in Stone Age caves. You will create your characters, their actions and the world that they inhabit, from the resources of your own mind.

It has been said that what publishers are looking for is 'the same thing, with a different twist' and there is a lot of truth in this. 'The same thing' is the basic structure of the book. Crime novels depend upon the solving of a crime; romances on the vicissitudes of love; in thrillers a hero or heroine overcomes a threat; historical novels try to recreate the past; modern novels reflect society and the complex interplay of people and careers – and so on through science fiction, horror, fantasy and the rest. These are the basic 'genres' of which you probably have heard and, unless you are exceptionally creative and talented (in which case you do not need this book), you will probably elect to work in one of them.

Yet to set your work apart, you must have the 'something different' of your own: the slant, the twist, the background which is your speciality and which will mark your manuscript out from all the others on the pile. This is where your individuality comes in.

This book sets out to help you to make the most of this 'individuality', in three ways. First, to help you to tap into that unique resource by looking at how imagination works, and how to fire it, both for yourself and for your potential readership. There is some technical information in this section, but, once you master it, you will be able to apply it to everything you write.

Secondly it seeks to show you ways to make the most of the knowledge that you have. Writers are often to urged to 'write about what you know', but this is not always the good advice it seems. Readers need a world with which they can associate, either imaginatively or from their own experience, and also one which seems intrinsically interesting or glamorous. If 'what you know' is either too technical or too commonplace to fulfil these requirements – and this may be true whether your world is tax accountancy or welding, millinery or office filing work – too much 'writing about what you know' may not be such a good idea. If you are an air-hostess, work in high-powered advertising or have lived twenty years in Outer Mongolia, it may be different, but even then the realities of such a life are often less interesting and glamorous than people tend to think.

I believe that the converse advice might be more suitable. Never write from a position of ignorance. It is not acceptable to make things up when accurate information about them is available. When you discover what you need to know (and this book seeks to help you to recognize what that might be in the case of your own writing), it is then possible to find it out, either by experience or research. Then you can use your 'knowledge' to give colour to your work. This book also aims to help you to make the most of knowledge of a different sort, by recognizing 'hidden messages': information we take in about the world about us or the people that we meet and often do not know that we possess. Once you have identified some of these 'messages', you can include them in your writing to give your plot more verve, your settings more impact and your characters more life and depth.

Lastly, the book contains some suggestions about plotting, dialogue and style. Again, there is technical information here, but much of this you probably already know instinctively. However, most people who do not have linguistic training do not recognize how much they know about the way words work until it is pointed out to them. You may find it surprising how the exploitation of a few technical devices can alter a sentence or paragraph and carry messages to the reader which are almost subliminal.

In order to put these ideas into practice and so make them clear, you will find in the text a number of suggested activities. There are four main types, as follows.

- Simple 'check-points' (to allow you to reflect on how the ideas in the text relate to your own work in progress).
- Illustrative quotations drawn from published novels to help you to analyse how techniques outlined in this book are used by well-known authors in their work. Please note that these extracts are deliberately drawn from a wide range of periods and genres, and there will probably be some that do not appeal to you. Nevertheless, it is recommended that you work through them all and try to profit by analysing the techniques. After all, these works have all been published with considerable success!
- Five-minute 'exercises' with pen and paper with which to practise and analyse suggested techniques.
- 'Concrete imagination' activities and visualization techniques. These are a little different. You will, of course, find detailed instructions in the text, but you may find it more helpful to make a tape recording of these so that you are able to concentrate entirely on the visualization without having to refer back to the written word (this is rather a bother to begin with, but people have found it well worth the effort in the end). In your first attempts with this type of activity it is probably best if you do not try to work with scenes that you have already written or planned in detail. This may sound perverse, since the object of the book is to help you with that very novel, but you will inevitably be influenced by decisions you have already made, rather than explore what the technique holds for you. Once you have mastered it, however, you can then tailor the activity and if necessary record another tape to match the particular requirements of your own writing.

These four activities are central to the book. Please take a pen and paper and try them out, even if you think you know what is involved. It is really not enough to work them in your head! Merely thinking about mental exercise will not help you to write, any more than merely thinking about physical exercise will make you fit and trim. You have, after all, already expended time and money on this book in the hope that it will offer something 'practical'. Do ensure that you make the most of it.

At the end of several chapters you will find a 'worksheet page'. This is primarily intended for beginners, or those who welcome more structured and detailed advice, and offers step-by-step guidance on using the techniques outlined elsewhere in the book to build up the various elements of narrative and integrate them into a whole. Naturally, if you are well advanced with your manuscript or are an established writer anyway these sections may not be applicable to you – unlike the other exercises, they are not central to the book. (On the other hand, you might find them worth a glance, as they may offer useful discipline or even occasionally be a source of new ideas.)

Before we begin to examine these techniques in detail, it is important to understand one fundamental principle on which this book is based. I call it 'the reader contract' and it underlies all the advice and every exercise that follows.

THE READER CONTRACT: WHAT A WRITER UNDERTAKES TO DO

Almost every would-be writer dreams of getting 'a contract' to fulfil, but, in fact, you have one, the moment you begin. It is a contract, not with a publisher, but with any potential reader that you have. Many people,

when asked, 'Why are you writing this novel?', will answer 'For myself.' That is, of course, a perfectly honourable position and has the advantage that, given reasonable application, success is guaranteed. Once the novel is written, the thing is done: the writer has no need to publish it. However, the truth is that in their heart of hearts most authors hope to find a publisher, which means that they are really writing for other people. Naturally, your work must satisfy yourself, that is almost a prerequisite, but ultimately it must satisfy the reader too.

Indeed, a mistake that many beginners make is to write a story purely for 'themselves' and expect a publisher to welcome it. It does not occur to them that the written word, like the spoken word, requires two parties to fulfil its task. It may be liberating to stand on a mountain top and shout into the wind or to sing in the bath, but in order to communicate you need a listener. In the same way, a writer needs a reader before his or her words can be said to convey anything at all. It is a two-way contract. You expect your reader to devote time and attention to your work, in preference to other things that he or she might do. More than that, ultimately you require somebody – the reader or someone acting on his behalf – to part with hard-earned cash for the privilege of reading what you write, again in preference to other things. Your reader is entitled to have certain expectations in return.

Think of your own expectations when you read a novel. Do not try to apply this list to what you write for now – this is what this book will help you do – but try to see it from the reader's point of view. Your expectations probably read something much like this:

> This is the author's own, original work. It is not heavily based on other people's work, nor a pale copy of some best-selling book that I've already read.

The story will keep me interested until the end. It will not tail off in the middle nor wander off on the author's hobby horse, nor will the plot take half the volume to begin.

The world in this story is consistent in itself and I will be able to imagine it. It will not flout known historical facts nor the laws of physics (though in a science fantasy it may have different laws of physics of its own, in which case they will be spelt out, credible and applied throughout). Fictional landscapes will be geographically consistent (the door which leads into the hall on p.11 does not open into the dining-room on p.93) and there is sufficient information on the page to allow me to mentally reconstruct this world and the characters who inhabit it.

All characters spring directly from this imaginary world. They are not caricatures of persons unknown to me, tributes to the author's friends and relatives nor opportunities for settling old scores.

These characters conform to what I know of human psychology, so that I can imaginatively relate to them. They have strengths and failings, characteristic traits and generally act from recognizable motives of some kind. This is true even if they are rabbits, as in *Watership Down*, or trolls in an imaginary world, as in Terry Pratchett. Occasionally in horror stories I may tolerate 'inhuman' characters, with no recognizable personality nor moral code, almost invariably as machines or aliens. However, these are mere instruments of the plot; I am not expected to take an interest in their fate, only the threat they pose to creatures more recognizably like myself.

Characters will speak as I recognize that people might genuinely speak in the situations arising in the plot, and there will be slight individual differences so that I can tell major characters apart. They will not all speak in exactly the same way as the author does.

The plot will not require me to believe in strange coincidences nor sudden changes of character, even if these have been experienced to the author in real life.

There will be sufficient plot, and it will not be wholly predictable. The structure of the story will be sufficiently clear for me to follow what is happening, even if, as in a thriller or a mystery, I do not know exactly what is causing it nor how different parts of the story interrelate. I shall, however, discover all this before the end.

The style in which the book is written makes it easy for me to read on. It does not drag on at the same old pace nor gallop so fast that I struggle mentally to keep up with it. I shall not be baffled by lots of words I do not know (unless they are explained immediately in the text) nor held up by an impenetrable dialect. Errors of usage will not interrupt my imaginative flow.

Lastly, and perhaps most importantly of all,

I bring with me my own picture of the world, and – unless you tell me otherwise – I shall apply it to your imaginary one.

Of course, as a would-be author, it is daunting to try to think about all this at once, but your novel represents a huge investment of your time and energy. If you can learn to think about this 'reader contract' and apply it as you write, you will have gone a long way towards avoiding months of disappointment and rejection slips. Remember, the publisher or agent to whom you send your work is only the first 'reader' that you meet, and, although obviously commercial instinct enters into it, success depends on your fulfilling this implied contract. Indeed, so-called 'commercial instinct' is often based on it. The publisher's business is to sell books: his or her interest is primarily in what the reader thinks.

WHAT IS A NOVEL?

If we look carefully at this 'reader contract' we shall see that, in fact, it can be said to offer a kind of definition of what a novel is, by contrast to other forms of prose. In the first place, it is fiction – 'the author's own unaided work'. It may be based on a real incident or on historic characters, but the detail of events and people in the story are the author's own imaginative reconstruction of the facts.

Secondly, it is not a short story, and for reasons other than mere length. A short story may be from 6,000 to 7,000 words in length, whereas a novel usually runs to something more than 60,000, and up to 200,000 for a blockbuster. Yet there are more subtle and fundamental differences than that.

The action in short stories, especially modern ones, usually takes place over a short span of time, frequently no more than a day or two at most, and often with a single, central incident. There is a single central character, although there may be several secondary ones, and the viewpoint of narration does not change. Within these confines there is no time for characters to change: the plot begins just before or at a significant moment of crisis or of change, traces the event, shows how it was resolved and hints at the long-term consequence. Any development in the central character can only be the realization of potential which was already latent – the character discovers inner strength or uses some known talent to resolve the plot. (It is important, even

in a short story, that the resolution of the problem requires some *effort*, physical or mental, from a character; events which resolve themselves by chance are rarely successful plots.) The mood of the story tends to be consistent or to change no more than once or twice, and therefore the narration can be successfully managed with no great variation in pace. Novels differ from all this in many ways.

1. In a novel, *setting is more significant*. Of course, in a short story the background matters too, but it is often sketched in, if it is present at all. In a novel it is an essential element. The reader contract requires that you create, not just an incident, but an entire 'world' which must be established sufficiently clearly and consistently to sustain a reader throughout hundreds of pages.

2. There is *scope for a greater cast of characters*. Short stories can carry only a few characters, but in a novel there may be a much larger cast, partly because the protracted action and fuller setting demand it, although minor characters must add something to the plot. There may even be more than one 'viewpoint character.' Even so, there is usually only one main protagonist.

3. In a novel *the central characters have time to develop* and to change. Events may sour them or they may be forced to take an uncharacteristic stance, but their characters are more completely formed.

4. There is *more scope for the vicissitudes of fortune*, too (although a 'happy coincidence' remains an unsatisfactory basis for a plot) and the resolution of conflict does not have to rely on the central character alone, although some effort from that character is still required.

5. *There may be subplots*, interwoven with the central plot or linked to it thematically in some way. The main plot cannot consist of one simple incident, but must offer a degree of complexity. Most novels can be said to have a theme, whereas short stories generally do not.

6. Lastly, because of its length and the diversity of parts, a novel requires *a variety of pace* and the ability to create and sustain *dialogue, differentiated for different speakers* in a way which a shorter piece does not.

A quick glance at the reader contract will show you that these are exactly the areas covered there. Let us apply all this to a book that you have read, before going on to consider these points in detail.

Five-Minute Exercise: Questionnaire

Think about the last book that you really enjoyed and one that you did not enjoy. Which of these criticisms, if any, would you apply to each of them:

The characters: • lacked reality • lacked empathy • lacked differentiation • there were too many characters
The background: • too much information • too little information • intrusive • incorrect information
The style was: • stilted • heavy • irritating • intrusive • long-winded
The dialogue was: • dated • boring • unconvincing
The plot was: • too slow • too slight • too dense • implausible • predictable • had internal inconsistencies
The pace was: • too slow • too fast • too even

CHECKPOINT

Which clauses of the reader's contract do you feel most confident of fulfilling? Which (be honest about this) will cost you the most effort to fulfil?

WHAT KIND OF WRITING?

There is one other matter of such importance that it should be mentioned here. What kind of novel will you choose to write? The range of possibilities is very wide, and novels varying enormously in genre, length and style are found on every library and bookshop shelf. In fact, the chances are, if you are reading this book, that you already have a chosen genre in mind. If not (or even if you have) there is one important principle to observe.

There is little point in attempting to write in any style or genre (that is, any type of story, adventure, romance, thriller or whatever) *which you do not read with pleasure for yourself.* This seems so obvious that it scarcely requires to be said, but a surprising number of 'beginning' authors do set out to produce the kind of book in which they do not themselves believe – light, popular romance is an obvious example – because they think that this offers the swiftest route to publication. (And yes, when I began, I fell into the self-same trap.)

It is not a good idea to do this for a number of reasons, not least that, even if it is accepted, you will not be very pleased with it. However, a manuscript written in this way is unlikely to succeed because editors are skilled in detecting insincerity, and so – more importantly – are the readers of such books. Writers who write less well but with more genuine feeling are likely to be preferred. What is more, if you are unfamiliar with a given genre you are unlikely to avoid either the more obvious pitfalls or the more obvious plots, and you may have no real idea of what your supposed market actually is, as opposed to what you think it is. This is so true of some of the major romance publishers that they actually provide tip-sheets for would-be authors, partly to help them but also to prevent people from sending in wholly unsuitable material.

Whatever genre of novel you choose to attempt, this book sets out to help you to apply the 'reader contract' to your writing, clause by clause.

2   SETTINGS

The world in this story is consistent in itself and I will be able to imagine it.

Reader contract

It may seem strange to begin by considering setting, as many would-be writers regard this as merely an unimportant background to the action. In fact, as we have already seen, it should be a good deal more than that – and there are four important reasons why.

WHY SETTINGS MATTER

Settings Ground Your Narrative in Time and Space

Every reality has its historical and geographical location, and therefore this is an essential element of a fictional reality too. This will govern facts, attitudes, style of dress and social conventions – even sometimes what is possible in what you write about. (You cannot blithely create a Victorian woman doctor, for example, although I once read a manuscript which did.) This is true whether you are writing gritty adventure stories or science fantasy – although the 'historical and geographical location' may be wholly imaginary. Even if your novel is set in the present and in a city or town much like your own, this will still have implications for your characters and influence how they think and what they do. Which brings us to the second point.

Settings Help to Create Character – Real or Fictional

Characters are partially determined by location, particularly in the reader's mind. Take a

character called Richard and place him on the polar ice cap with a couple of huskies, a tent and a sledge. Your reader already has certain expectations about the character and about the nature of the story. (Haven't you, yourself?) Take a character called Richard and make him librarian of a tiny library in a Cotswold village, and you have a different set of expectations.

Of course, as a writer you can use this for effect. Put the librarian on the ice floe or confine the Arctic explorer to the provincial book stacks and you may have the making of an interesting event. But the impetus derives, all the same, from what the reader expects of country librarians or Arctic trekkers. Did you for a moment, in your mental picture, suppose the two to be the same personality?

The contrast does not have to be so geographically extreme to 'lead' the reader to expectations in this way. Let us imagine two school leavers, potential victims in a detective plot. Kylie went to the local comprehensive, lives in a house on an estate and has a Saturday job. Deborah went to Ulbridge Ladies College, lives in Howlett Hall and spends Saturdays pursuing her hobby. Do you already have certain expectations? What is Kylie's job? Deborah's hobby?

The setting that you decide upon will usually dictate, to some extent, how your characters dress (assistants in a high street bank do not usually wear orange dungarees to work), how they speak, what they hope for and how they behave. Going back to the original Kylie and Deborah, can you hear their voices? One of the problems about a novel in which setting is *not* used in this way is that all the characters tend to speak like one another or, worse still, like you.

If this seems like typecasting of an obvious kind, perhaps it is – but it is certainly one that your readership will apply. Remember the reader's contract which says, 'I shall bring my own vision of the world unless you tell me otherwise'? Of course, you do not want your characters to be stereotypes, but, conversely, unless they spring from a 'real' imagined place, there is the risk that they will not have depth.

If you want to say, 'But my Kylie is a part-time motor mechanic, and Deborah breeds ferrets', you are showing signs of being a writer. Being aware of stereotypes is a first step to the avoiding of them and providing your characters with personalities that are individual and interesting. Yet the settings that you choose, in time and place, must partly mould the characters and their lives. Your Kylie and Deborah may be alike in many things – both bright, rebellious, selfish, go-ahead and fashionable – but they will still be very different. They will not dress, behave, speak nor think in the same way. Circumstances will have seen to that, even if they were twins, separated at birth. It is up to you, the author, to make us feel that truth. Equally, an elderly pigeon fancier in a home, or a devout nun in a convent does not casually become a murdering thief. Reconciling these two things might make a wonderful story, but only because we have some picture of what nuns and elderly pigeon fanciers are usually like.

Settings Often Offer the Basis for a Plot

If you look back over the preceding paragraphs, you will probably see the beginnings of several plots. Why was the murderer masquerading as a nun? Why was that nice, dull, unassuming man driven to the extremity of murder? What did Kylie see that puts her under threat? What happened to the librarian who found himself unfortunately stranded on an ice floe, and what circumstances put him there? And so on.

A good, if simple, way of creating a plot or sub-plot is to begin with a setting and put someone into it who does not entirely fit. This creates immediate tension, which is one of the first requirements of plot. In fact, if you think of novels you have read it may surprise you how often this 'tension' is a feature of the plot. From Stephen King to Dickens – Austen, Le Carré, Rankin, Pritchard, Sharpe – there are 'misfits' in every one of them, in every genre and in every age.

Settings Can Offer Individuality

Lastly, but no less importantly, settings can provide the 'something different' which marks out your novel from others on the pile. This is where experience and research come in, and (this is important enough to repeat) remember that one should not write from ignorance. If you are writing about a real place which you used to know be particularly careful about this. Your reader may know more about modern Poland than you do, especially if your information is based on a visit made some time ago.

If your work is historical, make sure that the geography you envisage was correct at the time of your novel. It is all too easy to get this wrong and blandly refer to buildings, streets and other features which were not there at the time of the story. Journeys seem to offer peculiar difficulties. If your hero is about to catch a train, ensure that there was one, at that date, from Glasgow to London on Thursday afternoon at half-past two in the afternoon in June – or whatever combination of events your plot requires. It is not enough simply to make it up. Out there somewhere, among your potential readership there are people who will not only know all this, but could tell you what kind of train it was and possibly even the name of the engine that was pulling it.

Even modern settings may be difficult, because technology moves so fast these days. This can pose especial traps if you are writing about a commercial world that you have recently left. To take an obvious example: in large offices typewriters are unlikely to be seen, and even faxes have been largely supplanted by email now.

CREATING A SETTING: UNDERSTANDING YOUR IMAGINATIVE STYLE

So, given that the setting is essential, how can you effectively create one as the basis for your imaginary world? There are two routes to achieving this: through imaginative research or through personal memory, and at this point it may help to look at some psychological discoveries that may be of importance to any writer hoping to create or to recreate a scene.

Clearly, both imagination and memory are functions of the brain, but recent study seems to show that scientifically they are more than this. The two functions are very close indeed. When a person is asked to remember an event and later asked to imagine something similar which he has not experienced, tests show that the same areas of the brain literally 'light up' in either case. This is of great importance to the writer, since other tests have shown that there are actually different 'styles' of imagination and memory. (Incidentally, this is the result of serious scientific research, not pop psychology, although, of course, we can only summarize it here. If you wish to investigate it

more thoroughly you will find a book list at the end.) This insight has transformed the way business management and education conduct their training practices, and you can apply it to your writing too.

Briefly, research has shown that there are four strategies for remembering or imagining a scene. We know that the outer part of the brain is divided into cortices, each cortex dealing with a different kind of information – and with modern technological advances it is now possible to discover which areas we use when acts of imagination and memory take place. It appears that we use the same areas as we employ when processing the functions of seeing, hearing and feeling (both physical and emotional) and cognitive thought, respectively, and so we may regard these as the four imaginative 'strategies', each using a different area of the brain. All of us, unless we suffer from a disability, are capable of using all of them, but most people rely most heavily on only one or two, unless required to do otherwise:

- 'visual' thinkers remember or imagine most readily what they *see*; this uses the 'visual' area of the brain;
- 'audial' ones rely more heavily on what they *hear*; this activates a different area of the brain;
- some people remember what they physically *feel* (texture, touch, space, movement and emotional attitude – and, for our purposes, smell and taste as well, although these are actually processed in slightly different but related, areas of the brain); this is called the 'kinaesthetic' style, although the name is not very important here;
- finally, some people use more *abstract strategies*, by trying to recall things 'intellectually'. They attempt to reconstruct a scene by using logic and looking for

measurement, comparisons, explanation, order and effect; this is called the 'cognitive' strategy.

Incidentally, none of this suggests that one 'style' is better or worse than any other, just that different individuals think in different ways as a first resource. If you are a visual thinker, and you are trying to recall some event, it may surprise you to discover that someone else attempting to remember the same thing will go about it in a completely different way.

WHY IS THIS IMPORTANT TO A WRITER?

This matters when you are writing a narrative, because it is natural to use the strategy that works for you. So, for example, if you are visually inclined, you will tend to describe a scene in terms of what you see. However, some of your potential readers are more influenced by what they hear: if you do not ever mention sounds at all, it is obvious that your 'picture' will not work so well for them. Or vice versa, naturally, and the same is true of all the other 'styles'.

There is the old advice, 'write about what you can see, what you can hear and what you can smell', which you may have been given at school. It seems that the advice was good, even if a little limited. Perhaps one should now add, 'include a bit about reason, measurement and cause'.

For instance, suppose that you wish to conjure up a scene in which a wet dog comes into the room. You can describe the dog's

The Brain

Recent research into the structure of the brain has revealed that there are actually different sections (cortices) which specialize in dealing with these four different kinds of stimulus. If you stimulate one particular brain cell in one part of the brain you will always trigger the same memory – pictures in the visual cortex, sounds in the audial cortex, feeling and sensation in the kinaesthetic cortex and explanation (Why was I there? When was that?) in the cognitive cortex (sometimes called the 'construct route' to memory.) If you want your reader to imagine a similar event, that is the portion of the brain he will use.

There is still some disagreement as to exactly how many cortices there are. There certainly appear to be small, specialized areas dealing with smell and taste, and there may, for instance, be some physical interrelation between colour and vibration and the kinaesthetic sense. Nevertheless, for our purpose, these four styles will do.

More importantly from the writing point of view, it appears from brain-scanning experiments that – although all of us lay down these memories in exactly the same way, unless we have some physical or mental disability – different people habitually access different cortices for preference. Most people seem to rely on only two and will not actively bring the others into play unless the first-choice attempt to remember or imagine fails.

This may explain why different witnesses to the same event may have entirely different though genuine 'memories' of it, as any policeman or barrister will tell you. Memory is not of fact, but of the brain's reconstruction of the fact – a kind of imagination, in a word.

bedraggled appearance, and that will work for approximately a quarter to a half of your potential readership. Have it shake itself, giving off wet drops and a damp-dog smell, and you have caught the imagination of another group – more if you make it patter as it comes in and so bring audial components into play. If it is made clear how the animal got wet you satisfy the cognitive thinker, who would probably also like to know what kind of dog it was. All these effects, of course, may be achieved at once:

> A large, black spaniel came bounding in, its wet fur full of sand and giving off the gamey odour of damp dog. It shook itself with short, sharp flicks, then stood there panting hopefully.

This may not be a very good example, but no doubt you can see the principle. You will perhaps also recognize that, apart from stimulating the imagination of readers who have different styles, the incorporating of all the elements makes the scene more real for everyone. Unless we have some handicap, we all have access to all these strategies, but often do not use them unless we are required to do so.

In fact, if we are unexpectedly presented with a sight, a scent or a taste, it will often immediately trigger a host of memories. Marcel Proust was right: the flavour of warm jam tart may take you in imagination to a kitchen long ago, or the smell of gym shoes conjure up your old school locker room. As a writer you obviously cannot reproduce these scents and tastes, but you can allude to them. As with any technique, it is possible to overuse the trick, but used sparingly and for important scenes it has an effect which the reader often does not recognize.

In order to make the most of this, it helps to discover which of the four imaginative styles comes most naturally to you so that you can then make a specific effort to include the others in your work from time to time. You have just been imagining, I hope, an unexpected encounter with a wet dog. Ask yourself, for instance, which of the elements given here most enabled you to create an image of the scene? Visual? Audial? Kinaesthetic? Or a purely abstract conception? At what point did it become the most real for you?

The exercises which follow are designed to help you to discover what strategies you use in summoning up a scene. Try to work them through, because the answers may surprise you. Your instinctive imaginative style may not be what you thought it was at all.

Five-Minute Exercise: Finding Your Preferred Style

Take a piece of paper and pen or pencil (it is better not to use a computer for this exercise), find a quiet spot to work, and close your eyes. This is to eliminate, as far as possible, stimuli from outside sounds and sights which may trigger specific memories. The idea here is to discover how, left to yourself, you gain access to imagination and recall. Then give yourself three minutes – using a timer if you have one – to remember, as far as possible, your first day at school. When the time is up, open your eyes and, for the remaining two minutes, scribble down whatever comes to mind. *Do not attempt to structure what you write* – that would be imposing a 'construct' on your thoughts – this is for nobody but you. When you have finished writing (not before, what matters here is what you choose to write) refer to the checkpoints on p.20.

CHECKPOINT 1

Look at what you have written in the exercise. Is it primarily concerned with what was on the walls, the colour of the chairs, a picture of children, toys or books? If so, you probably rely most heavily on visual impression in your novel-writing too.

Or was the strongest memory of something that you heard – the teacher calling out your name, or welcoming you into the class, speaking to someone in the playground, hearing a tone of voice, listening to the piano or a song? In that case, the audial strategies are paramount for you. Note that this does not depend on being musical – simply that you learned early to rely on what you heard.

Did you remember chiefly something that you did or felt – perhaps your insecurity? Or did you conjure up the space: where your desk was situated or the general ambience of the room? People who recall information such as 'it was a bright and airy room' or 'I remember feeling very overawed' are choosing chiefly kinaesthetic prompts.

If your account of your first day gives explanation or external fact – where the school was situated, why you could not see, the reason you were feeling as you did – this indicates a 'construct' strategy. The same thing is also true if you either attempted to apply the information in the previous paragraphs and found yourself accessing every type of memory in turn, or 'switched off' from the exercise, telling yourself that it was all too long ago and was not relevant. If that is what you did, your reliance on your intellect alone is likely to permeate your fiction writing too. Remember that your reader may not think like you do.

Most people working through this exercise discover that they do, indeed, rely most heavily on one or two of the imaginative strategies, and it may come as a surprise to discover that other people use quite different methods of imagination and recall. (It is particularly interesting to try this with a group – the differing kinds of memory may astonish you.)

CHECKPOINT 2

You may wish at this point to look at something you have written previously – perhaps a short story or an extract from your novel. Find a descriptive paragraph and apply the same criteria to it. Is it describing mostly what you see, what you hear or what you feel: the visual, audial or kinaesthetic styles? Or does it suggest a mostly 'cognitive' strategy?

Now try to adapt just one sentence of the passage by adding, in a single phrase, one of the elements that was missing earlier. It is, of course, not necessary to do this every time – that would be mechanical and could quickly become counterproductive – but the effect of using this technique occasionally can be remarkable. If you train yourself to 'see' your mental scenes with all four of your strategies you will convey a sense of reality to your readership which they will recognize, often without really knowing why.

METHODS FOR DEVELOPING ALL YOUR LATENT STYLES

Once you have discovered which styles of thought come most naturally to you, it is helpful to practise using the others from time to time, so that you can use all the routes available to stimulate the imagination of your readership. Here are some tried and tested techniques for activating each of these strategies in turn. You may find there is nothing particularly new to you in the suggestions – different authors have sworn by all of them, over the years – and you will probably find one or two which accord most naturally with your thinking style. Perversely, however, it may be the others that you need to practise most, for

The Cortices

Here for future reference is a checklist of what each cortex is related to:

- The visual cortex deals with what we see – such things as colour, shape, the individual elements of a scene – and most of us rely on this information very much.
- The audial cortex deals with sound: noises, tunes, harmony, natural sounds and the pitch, volume and intonation of the human voice. Again, most of us process information in this way.
- The kinaesthetic area is a little more diffuse, but in essence it deals with feeling, both physical and emotional: cold, heat, fear, love, spatial relationships, and – for our purposes – taste and smell as well.
- The construct or cognitive area of the brain processes information by what we may roughly call 'intellect' and is concerned with order, reason, explaining, interpreting and classifying things. This means that construct thinkers tend to make mental lists, they like to categorize and define and often respond to abstract symbolism and comparisons with parallel events.

reasons we have already touched upon. It may be helpful, therefore, to work your way through all of these in turn.

OBSERVATION NOTEBOOKS

Many writers find it helpful to keep an 'observation notebook' in which they can record impressions and scenes as they encounter them. This is a useful way to use a bus or train journey, for example, noting down details of people or places that you see. The details of a

bus-shelter – the shape, the colour of the seats, if there are any, advertisements, graffiti, discarded cans, the pattern of the rain on its roof – these things will all make a useful atmospheric bank for future writing, and, at the same time, sharpen your observational powers. Clearly this is a purely visual activity, but once you are confident with that, you can deliberately draw on other strategies as well: for example, by trying to capture the sounds, smells or temperature of the scene.

Apply a similar technique to sound. Find yourself in a familiar place, where it is safe and close your eyes. Now try to concentrate exclusively on sound. Listen for things you otherwise might miss – distant traffic noises, people moving chairs, the background ticking of a clock. Try to concentrate until you have identified a least half a dozen different sounds. Decide which would most instantly conjure up the atmosphere of place. If you are not an 'audial' thinker you may find this difficult to do at first, not least because the language has few words for variation in the realm of sounds.

CONCRETE VISUALIZATION

Another kind of activity, bringing 'feelings' into play, is a kind of concrete visualization. It is impossible to describe this adequately without working through the method and so it is suggested that you try the following.

For this, you will not require to write to begin with; simply to sit in a quiet place and close your eyes. Think about a scene that you know well: your own home or place of work are good subjects to use for first attempts. Imagine standing at the entrance, really work at 'seeing' the door, and then reach out in your imagination and open it, however you normally do that. Try to conjure up the texture as you touch it and, as you open the door, be aware of what you are standing on, the feel of the surface beneath your feet. Look left and be aware of what you see. Try to evoke as much detail as possible. Then, in the same way, look to the right. Reach out and mentally touch something, trying to evoke the feeling in your fingertips as they encounter whichever object you have selected. Is it warm, cold, soft, grainy, yielding? Try to recreate the sensation as clearly as you can. Then walk on, trying to imagine objects as you pass and your own movement through the space, until you reach another door. Then stop, open your eyes and try to recall as many of those sensations as you can.

At this stage you may wish to write your ideas down, so that you can refer to them again. Some people also like to tape these instructions too, so that they can concentrate more fully on the experience. You may find it helpful, after you have tried this out, to walk yourself physically through the space you chose and compare the real experience with your imagined one. When you have done this several times, preferably choosing a different place each time, you can begin to apply the same technique to imaginary scenes and thus to the setting for your book.

MAKING A DIAGRAM OR MAP

Another method, drawing on the cognitive strategy, is to create a map of your imagined place. If you have a setting in your mind, try jotting down a simple plan of it, marking in the imaginary buildings, bus stops, churches, roads, whatever is important to your tale. Do the same thing for any building you create. For most authors, this exercise is best undertaken after the visualization process described above, otherwise the map dictates the setting, rather than the reverse. However, creating such a plan will prevent problems with 'consistent geography', such as that of the moving door we mentioned earlier.

KEEPING A WRITER'S DIARY: TAPES AND CARDS

Whichever techniques work best for you, it is probably a good idea to begin the habit of writing a few minutes every day. Many professional authors swear by this, and it is certainly a useful discipline. The first requirement for being a writer is to write, and this is a start, even if only for five minutes at a time. First thing in the morning is usually recommended, but those who have busy schedules may find this difficult, so any time when you can set aside a few moments will do. (My own favourite time is in the bath.) A pencil is probably the best medium for this exercise, as it moves smoothly across the page and you can erase or edit it at will. However, use anything, provided that you write.

The important thing is to keep writing for a specific length of time, which need not be long at this stage. Even two minutes can be valuable. What you write is not significant. It can be anything you wish, notes for a story, the events of yesterday (hence the phrase 'a writer's diary') or a simple stream of consciousness. The important thing is to keep the pencil moving at all times. If you cannot think of anything to write, then write 'I cannot think of anything to write' until inspiration strikes. Sometimes just following your thoughts can lead to surprising new ideas and, when you are thinking productively, it is often hard to keep up with the flow! It is also, of course, possible to use the diary as a way of trying out any of the techniques or exercises suggested here.

Again, this activity can be adapted to suit your thinking style. Audial thinkers may prefer to dictate their diaries to a tape or simply speak the words aloud to themselves as they go along. The very act of hearing what you write can alter the rhythm and balance of the words, and many authors practise this technique. Some people prefer to use stacks of card rather than a diary, on the basis that not only is this more convenient – you can carry a few cards anywhere – but it also permits them to separate and file their ideas. This particularly suits people who like to move things physically – the kinaesthetic group – who may also prefer to use differently coloured cards for different moods, and those who favour cognitive strategies, since they can organize material as they go.

CHECKPOINT 3

Think back to that exercise in Chapter 1 in which you looked at a novel that you enjoyed and one that you disliked. When you consider your responses there, which 'imaginative strategies' do your comments translate into?

This may be more difficult to do at first, but it can be illuminating when you see the connection. For instance, 'there was too much dialogue' (too audial), 'not enough description' (not visual enough), 'cardboard characters/not enough action' (not sufficiently kinaesthetic), 'made mistakes' or 'didn't hang together' (weak 'cognitive' sense). Do your tastes match your natural imaginative style? Or do you seem to prefer books that require you to use imaginative strategies that you do not usually call upon? What does this tell you about your own likely strengths and weaknesses?

USING YOUR SETTING IN THE NARRATIVE

Having created a vivid setting in your mind, it is extremely tempting to begin your writing by introducing your reader to the scene you have imagined with a long passage of descriptive prose. However, this is rarely a good idea and many 'how to write' guides suggest that it should never be attempted. As usual, there is a degree of truth in this, but, on the other hand,

it immediately rules out most of Thomas Hardy, as well as a good many contemporary authors (look at Sebastian Faulks' *Birdsong*, for example, or the opening of Iris Murdoch's *The sea, the sea*). Perhaps the best advice is to avoid these long, introductory, descriptive passages unless you intend to use them for a particular effect. For instance:

1. The landscape, or setting, is such a strong ingredient that it is almost a character in itself. This is the case with Hardy, for example, and some adventure stories (Wilbur Smith's South African series is a case in point), where the environment is particularly harsh.

2. In situations where the chief character is an outsider to or in conflict with the setting, which is in itself extreme – like our trekker in the library, above, or in many science fiction and adventure novels – so that this clash may be an important element of the plot. Le Carré, Patrick O'Brien, L. Ron Hubbard and Tom Clancy have all used this technique. Douglas Adams, in *Dirk Gently's Holistic Detective Agency*, also begins with a dramatic landscape, this time for comical contrast and effect.

3. Finally, this technique can be applied in 'literary' novels where a poetic or elegiac mood is required.

Even in these cases, great caution is required. Research into reader preferences suggests that, unless the writing is particularly fine, many will not pursue a story that begins with long, descriptive paragraphs – sometimes even when it *is* particularly good. It is worth noting, too, that even when such paragraphs occur in the body of the narrative, large numbers of readers reported that they simply skim read them or even skip them altogether. If this is true, your careful mood-building may easily be lost.

Study Box

Here are two quite lengthy descriptive openings. Each describes a setting, but note how it is also used to create dramatic contrast to the coming storyline. Faulks's novel of the First World War begins with an evocation of a placid, respectable town, but the author uses place names ('Amiens' and 'the river Somme') to cue our knowledge of the slaughterhouse to come. In the second piece, the cheerful clatter of Christmas is used as contrast to the tension and rigidity of the woman in the cab – a cab to which we are alerted within the first ten words. Note also how the first piece employs visual and cognitive strategies – with mathematical allusions – while the second uses sound, pictures and kinaesthetic cues to create the atmosphere.

The boulevard du Cange was a broad, quiet street that marked the eastern flank of the city of Amiens. The wagons that rolled in from Lille and Arras to the north made directly into the tanneries and mills of the Saint-Leu quarter without needing to use this rutted, leafy road. The town side of the boulevard backed onto substantial gardens which were squared off and apportioned with civic precision to the houses they adjoined. On the damp grass were chestnut trees, lilac and willows, cultivated to give shade and quietness to their owners. The gardens had a wild, overgrown look and their deep lawns and bursting hedges could conceal small clearings, quiet pools and areas unvisited even by the inhabitants, where patches of grass and wild flowers lay beneath the branches of overhanging trees.

Behind the gardens the river Somme broke up into small canals ...

Sebastian Faulks, *Birdsong*

It was Christmas Eve in New York City. The cab slowly made its way down Fifth Avenue. The traffic was heavy and the sidewalks were jammed with last-minute Christmas shoppers, homebound office workers, and tourists anxious to glimpse the elaborately trimmed store windows and the fabled Rockefeller Center Christmas tree.

It was already dark and the sky was becoming heavy with clouds, an apparent confirmation of the forecast for a white Christmas. But the blinking lights, the sounds of carols, the ringing bells of sidewalk Santas, and the generally jolly mood of the crowd gave an appropriately festive Christmas Eve atmosphere to the famous thoroughfare.

Catherine Dorman sat bolt upright in the back of the cab.

Mary Higgins Clark, *Silent Night*

So, if long, introductory descriptions are not usually a good thing, how can the author make the setting clear? Usually by beginning with a character and action, and permitting the setting to disclose itself.

All the same, readers must have enough information in the first few paragraphs to be able to create the mental scene, remembering that, in this country, this is likely to be a modern, British city, unless you instruct them otherwise. So, if your novel is set in medieval Italy, you will have to intersperse the action with enough clues to create the background from the outset, since there are few things more irritating than to find that the mental picture, once created, has to be utterly revised.

Even so, a few, well-chosen details can sometimes conjure up the scene more effectively than pages of description. Mention the sun's heat, a campanile, the horseman's purple velvet hat and cloak, and you can save the dust, smells and all the rest for later on.

The same advice applies through the narrative. Keep feeding your setting in like this throughout, a little at a time, weaving it in whenever possible. You do not need to describe 'a big, deal table in the centre of the room', if your character is about to walk to it. Simply write, 'He strode to the big, deal table in the centre of the room' instead. The reader will internalize that picture without realizing that this is a description of the scene at all.

The reverse, of course, is also true. In a long section of dialogue, action or stream-of-consciousness it is sometimes helpful to jog the reader's memory of the scene, where this is all supposed to be taking place. This may be as simple as, 'Somewhere in the street above, a car horn blared.' Just a small reminder of the setting, but such things can make a huge difference to pace, for instance, and help to bring alive a scene which is not reading well.

It is a good discipline in creating any scene throughout the book, to shut your eyes and do a concrete visualization exercise on it. If you force yourself to visualize the room, evoke the scents and smells, the sounds and the atmosphere, the setting will become alive for you. If

Study Box

Look at the two following quotations, both taken from the first page of a novel. The first is an opening paragraph. The character acts, and so discloses the setting.

> Nicholas Elliott ... pushed open the inner door of the Cathedral porch and heard the singing. It was early, not much after eight in the morning, and outside the Cathedral there had been no sound but the wind and a few gulls looping, crying round the tower ...
>
> Joanna Trollope, *The Choir*

In the second, details of the setting are deliberately revealed by degrees. The view of roofs, the dusty chair, the peeling plaster, the coffee, the fact that this is Paris – as well as the dress and briefcase of the visitor – only emerge as the characters interact.

'All the ones I meet are,' said the courier. He too stopped looking across the humpty-backed rooftops, and as he turned away from the window he noticed a patch of white plaster on his sleeve. He brushed it petulantly as though Paris was trying to get at him. He pulled at his waistcoat – a natty affair with wide lapels – and then picked at the seat of the chair before sitting down ...

I pushed the coffee pot to him. 'Real coffee,' he said. 'The French seem to drink only instant coffee nowadays.' Thus reassured of my decorum he unlocked the briefcase that rested upon his knees.

> Len Deighton,
> *An Expensive Place to Die*

it is not, how can you expect it to be real for your readership? Sometimes, if you are writing about a different period or a way of life you are not familiar with, this will bring home to you what elements you still need to research (*see* the Five-Minute Exercise opposite).

FINDING BACKGROUND INFORMATION

When you do discover areas of ignorance by attempting to visualize your setting in this way, where can you find the information you require? Obviously, reference books are a good place to start, and the bibliography of one book can lead you to another. Your library will help you in your search, but there is no substitute for owning a few of the most useful books for your selected period and geographical location. There is an amazing range of non-fiction material available on everything from histories of false-teeth to Celtic recipes.

Contemporary documents are an excellent resource, if you are researching history. Pay particular attention to contemporary memoirs, diaries, collections of letters and autobiographies. Even if these do not touch on the particular events that happen in your novel, they will give you a clearer picture of the times. Even account books and commercial correspondence may be helpful here. Newspapers are probably the easiest contemporary documents to find, giving you not only information about the major events of a period, and often pictures too, but also such things as letter pages and advertisements, which can give you more of the 'flavour' of an age than any number of simple facts. Again, there are compilation volumes available and libraries often have their own collections, which are increasingly on microfiche and the Internet (but *see* below). Magazines can be valuable as well.

Photographic records, where such things

Five-Minute Exercise

Try this exercise, which calls on cognitive strategy, to show you how this works. Look around the room that you are in and decide what would have been different in it or its equivalent, twenty years ago. Fifty? A hundred? Start with the floor and work upwards, not forgetting the ceiling and light fixtures. Choose one of those periods and try to do a visualization of the scene.

exist, or – failing that – other pictorial representations such as paintings and sketches can give you more information about a period than a thousand words. Volumes of historic, local photographs are now available, if these are relevant to you. Maps and even tourist information brochures can help if you are writing about a place you do not intimately know. Be careful of historical locations here: buildings which appear in photographs or maps may not have been there when your narrative takes place. City archivists and local historians are usually happy to offer guidance in such matters, and companies occasionally have their own records, which some will let you see.

Museums and exhibitions are worth visiting if they cover any area which you write about. Most have excellent libraries and exhibits which are not on show and which you can often see if you write and explain what you require (the Imperial War Museum and the National Army Museum, for example). Curators and experts are often willing to help, so do not be afraid to ask. Any person with first-hand experience or expertise is probably the most valuable resource of all, if you are lucky enough to find him.

Naturally one can use the Internet to find things out these days, and an immense amount of information can be accessed in this way. However, it is important to recognize that its appearing on the web is no guarantee that an essay or article is reliable. Material on the Internet is only as good as the source that posted it there, so – while it can be a magnificent resource – it should be double-checked, unless it comes from a reputable source.

On-line chat rooms can put you in touch with enthusiasts and experts on an amazing range of topics too, most of whom are only too happy to answer any enquiries you may have.

Finally, if all else fails, most writers' magazines will give you the names and addresses of individuals or companies who will do research for you, for a fee, provided that you tell them exactly what you want to know.

This worksheet attempts to bring together a number of elements already outlined in the text. Some of the instructions may be found (in other forms) elsewhere, but they are repeated here for ease of reference. Avoid being self-critical at first, and simply allow the subconscious to 'get on with it'. However, please do not attempt the activity until you have worked through the preceding chapter and have already practised and are familiar with the appropriate techniques.

1. Begin with a concrete visualization exercise. Give yourself time for this, and if you need to open your eyes to note down one or two details, do so and then return to the activity. (You may find it helpful to tape these instructions, but otherwise read them one sentence at a time, and work on that before you move on to the next idea.) So close your eyes and allow your imagination to get to work. If you already have some ideas about this place, use them as a starting-point: this visualization should make them more 'concrete' in your mind – hence the name of this activity.

You are outside a building. This time make it one that occurs in your story – a central one if that is possible. Concentrate on the building. What is it made of? What shape is it? When, approximately, was it built? What stands on either side of it, if anything?

Now start to walk towards it. What is underneath your feet – gravel, concrete, grass? Go up to an entrance. Enter the building – how do you get in? As you go in, how big is the space that you are entering? What is the source of light and what can you see in front of you? To your left? Your right? Linger on this picture – if there is furniture, take it in piece by piece. Decide if there are windows, and if so, what is the view? Is there anything hanging on the walls? Another exit? If there is another room or space, explore. Don't forget to look up above your head. And down: what are you walking on – carpet, lino, floorboards, bare earth?

2. Once you have a clear and detailed picture in your mind, deliberately revisit it, and this time ask yourself what sounds and smells there are. Reach out and touch things as you pass, and be aware of texture, heat and cold, and how the floor feels underneath your feet.

3. Revisit the same scene, but at night. How is it lit, if at all, and what is different now?

4. This time, begin in the same way, but traverse the whole building from your entry point. This may mean going up, around or down and should give you some idea of scale. There is no need to take in the journey in such detail, but do glance about you as you go, and take in the ambience and general geography. Be aware of any other doors and – if possible – discover what's behind them. (If it is a huge building, and you go by lift, get off at one intermediate floor and have a look.)

5. Using this exploration as a basis, draw a small sketch map of the building as far as you are able to. You will probably discover in the course of this that there are areas that you don't know at all, or which you are still very unclear about. Don't force it, but remember that when you come to write, you can use the same technique again to explore these other areas as well.

6. If there were any items that were hazy in your imagination, either because you could not imagine them effectively, or because you did not know what was likely to be in the sort of place you were imagining, then this is an indication that your setting still needs work. Find more information from one of the sources listed in the text, and then try the exercise again.

7. If you did manage it successfully, try jotting down some of the details of your imagined scene, especially any details that came to you as a 'revelation'. Don't make this an opening passage, at least not yet, but write it as atmospherically as you can, so that you can dip into it later on, when some of the other elements have fallen into place.

3 CHARACTERS

All characters spring direct from this imaginary world (and) conform to what I know of human psychology, so that I can imaginatively relate to them.

Reader contract

THE IMPORTANCE OF CHARACTERS

The setting may be an essential background to your story, but the characters are what the novel is about. Even if the setting and incidents remained the same, it would be a different novel – or it ought to be – if the events that you describe were happening to someone else. Would-be writers do not always realize this. A workshop member once complained to me, 'I've got a good plot worked out, but I'm not sure exactly about the characters.' In other words, this was not anyone's 'story', the characters were merely a mechanism to let a plot unfold.

This is an easy mistake to make when setting out. (I fell into it myself, and received the rejection slip to prove it: 'this is an interesting and well-written story, but we do not know enough about the main character' – you have been warned.) Yet a moment's consideration will show us that the plot should spring from the characters, their lives and situations, otherwise the story is an extended anecdote which could have occurred to anyone who happened to be there. What makes a novel is the individual personality and motivation of the central characters.

DIFFERING 'LEVELS' OF CHARACTER

Of course, not all characters are equally important to the plot. It may be helpful to think of the characters as being in four 'levels' of significance.

First-level characters are those that are the most central to the plot, the people that the story is essentially about. In a novel there may be several: a conventional romance will necessarily have a hero and heroine, for instance, a thriller, a pursuer and the pursued. Even so, I suggest that you regard your story as having *one* lead character, the one with whom the audience can most sympathize and identify, with one or two other first-level characters surrounding him or her. This will assist you when considering the structure of the novel and give the narrative a unity.

Second-level characters: almost certainly there will be these in your story too – people who are essential to the plot and to the fabric of the whole, but who are not the central characters. Sometimes they supply the conflict or the obstacle in a romance or a contemporary drama: important colleagues, companions or co-conspirators in thrillers, detective or adventure novels. They may even be central figures in a sub-plot of their own, such as the romantic interest in an action plot.

Third-level characters may be of two kinds: some are lesser characters who occur throughout the plot, but in a background role. Others may appear quite briefly in the plot, being associated with a certain period or place but not appearing in the remainder of the story. Nonetheless, while they are on-stage, as it were, they may play a significant role in the mechanics of the plot: sometimes as the victim of a murder, for example, or sometimes by acting as a catalyst and doing something, either deliberately or unwittingly, which triggers subsequent events. They may create joy, unhappiness or tension, too, but not for the whole duration of the plot. This is what differentiates them from second-level characters.

Fourth-level characters are people who are much more incidental to the plot and will almost inevitably occur. Usually they are there because of what they do – they serve at table, keep a shop, command a battery of guns – and the tale would not be realistic if they were not there. Sometimes they may have important functions in the action (the cab-driver who drives the hero to the heist), but even there it is the function which is significant, rather than the personality of the character. This means that, in general, such characters do not require names; this is 'a cabbie' and not 'Freddie Jones', and this can be a quick way of deciding whether a particular character is a fourth-level one or not.

CREATING FIRST-LEVEL CHARACTERS

Naturally your first-level characters are the most important ones. They should be fully rounded, using all the techniques suggested later in this chapter, and your lead character at least should also show some signs of *development* in the course of the plot. This does not entail a total change of personality, but it does mean building on potential, whether by developing confidence, discovering reserves of courage and ingenuity or even becoming

cunning, disillusioned and cynical. It is particularly important that these characters truly inhabit your imagined world and are not thinly disguised portraits of your friends, relatives or enemies, who, after all, were shaped by a different reality.

It is often suggested that, in order to create rounded characters, you should create a check-list of important facts. This can be a useful exercise if properly applied, but it should be approached with care. Try out this activity to see why.

Five-Minute Exercise and Questionnaire

Look at this typical list of 'things to know' about a character:

- name, age, race and sex
- physical description
- job (what, where, how well paid, how does he/she get there?)
- important emotional ties (family, animals, friends, causes?)
- dress
- strengths and weaknesses
- likes and dislikes
- background (where born, educated?)
- habits and mannerisms
- home (where does he/she live? What does it look like? How well maintained?)
- important possessions

Now apply the list, not to one of your fictitious characters, but to someone real. Choose someone you know well, but not yourself: a friend, colleague, partner or relative. Which questions were the easiest to answer? Were there any that you had to guess? Which four answers seemed to sum up that person best? What can you learn from this about creating character?

You will see at once that this is not an exhaustive list and, in order to sum up the personality, you may wish to add questions of your own. It is sometimes suggested, for example, that in order to understand a character you need to know what kind of underwear he chooses and what he had for breakfast. However, note that your answers have emerged from your knowledge of the character, and not the other way about. The same principle applies equally when you are writing: a rounded character cannot satisfactorily be built simply by creating an arbitrary list of answers to the questionnaire. Nevertheless, as you build your character clearly in your mind, you should be increasingly able to decide the answers, in the same way as you did about your friend, and this is a useful check-list to apply in retrospect, to ensure that you do really know your character.

Some authors need to plan all this before they start. They think about their characters for days or weeks, jotting down notes about appearance and characteristics as they go. Only then do they begin to write. For others, all this detail may not be entirely clear until the narrative is under way: a character does not spring fully-armed from the imagination before they start, but begins as a generalized idea and emerges more and more clearly as they progress – just as we learn more about real people increasingly as we interact with them. You will have to discover for yourself which of these techniques works best for you.

There are advantages and disadvantages to both: preplanners, who decide on all the elements of personality in advance, will certainly avoid the trap of having someone act, as we say, 'out of character', but give themselves less flexibility and run the risk of having a character who seems too mechanical. On the other hand, those using a developmental strategy have to be prepared to rewrite and revise as unsuspected elements of character

arise. Learning more about the personality as you write can sometimes be an inconvenience: you realize that an action which you had planned as central to the plot is simply inconsistent with the character. If this happens to you, you should not despair, it is a first-class sign that your character is becoming real. Try to find some other way, perhaps an exterior force, to bring about the action you require, do not try to rewrite your character in retrospect.

Deciding upon which of these methods will work for you is largely a question of temperament; you may even find it useful to attempt them both, with different characters, to see which comes the more easily to you. Note, however, that the techniques for building character are much the same in either case, the difference is simply at what point you start to write.

We have already seen that setting is a useful starting point, so let us use this as a strategy for beginning to create a character.

CONCRETE VISUALIZATION

Again, you will need to close your eyes for this, and you may find it helpful to record the instructions on to a tape. If not, try to grasp the essentials of the exercise and work through it slowly, giving yourself time to concentrate on each question as it comes.

You are walking along the side of a building. This time make it one that occurs in your story. Concentrate on the building. What is it made of? What is underneath your feet – gravel, concrete, grass? What time of day is it? Is there any noise? Now turn the corner. What can you see? Find an aperture – door, window, anything – and go inside. Reach out and touch something as you do this. What texture do you feel? Now you are inside. What is your first impression? What is the source of light? What can you see in front of you? Look up – what can you see now? And down – what is underneath your feet now? What can you smell? Look right – is there another space? If so, what is it and what can you see there? And left? Listen. You can hear a voice. What is it saying? Go towards it until you can see the owner of the voice. What can you see? What is the person wearing? Doing? How old? Who is the person speaking to? What is he? Why is he here?

Unless you are a very abstract thinker, you should have found this picture fairly clear, especially if you have been practising the technique. Now try asking yourself the previous questionnaire again, this time about the character you 'saw'. How many of the questions can you answer easily? However, all these external things are only half of what matters in a character. As you will probably have realized from applying the questionnaire to someone that you know, the inner drives and motivation of a character are much more important than physical appearance and what the person wears.

CONCRETE VISUALIZATION

Do the previous visualization again, but this time, put yourself in the situation of the character. Look around the interior again, and this time try to see it through his eyes. What emotions and physical sensations is he feeling now? What made him speak the words you heard just now? Who was he talking to? What is he secretly thinking that he did not say?

Whatever your answers were, no doubt the principle is clear to you. Although the technique may take some practice to perfect, it is important that you have a real understanding of your first-level characters, not only in the way they act, but what impels them to behave in the way that they do. Deciding that your character drives a Porsche is not enough. Why does he do it? Is it expected of him? Is he showing off? Proving something to himself? Making up for being short and fat? Or does he simply love machinery? Even if you never tell the reader all of this, you have to understand his inner drives.

You can apply this principle of 'why' to everything he does and thus will learn to concentrate on motivation rather than merely on external facts, and this helps to create a fully rounded character. Of course, these motivations may not remain the same as the story progresses. On the contrary, as we noted earlier, a lead character should show signs of that development, and that is usually achieved by changed emotional priorities – by increased sensitivity to others, for example, or even by discovering self-worth. Everything that happens to a person helps to shape his motivation as to what he will do, say or think next. When an important event occurs in your narrative, always remember to ask yourself what effect this might have upon your central characters, even the ones not immediately involved.

If you are writing about a different period or society, some motivations may not be identical with our own. Do not forget the constraints of social convention, for example, or peer pressure, as we would call it now. This may be a powerful imperative, but how does your character react to this? If you write with a developmental strategy, you will obviously apply the concrete visualization technique as you go. If are a natural preplanner, you can still apply it briefly to key scenes before you start: choose incidents that occur throughout the book to help you to take account of those changing emotional priorities that lead to your character's development.

SOME TECHNIQUES FOR CREATING CHARACTER

Creating a rounded character in your imagination is an important step, but how does one convey this to the readership? There are a number of possible techniques, most of them based on the central axiom – 'don't tell – show!'

For most of us, impressions of character in real life are formed by watching people in action, listening to what they say, seeing how others react in their presence and hearing what is said behind their backs. The same things hold true in a narrative. This is the reason why most people find the visualization exercise an effective one. Of course, physical appearance is a factor too, but not nearly as important as some new authors suppose. Indeed, if you read carefully, you will see that some novelists give only the sketchiest picture of their lead character – a passing comment about hair colour and an implication of general attractiveness without much detail – precisely because this makes it easier for readers of all types to imaginatively put themselves into the character's shoes. If you are short, fat and balding it is still possible to cast yourself as the dashing, fearless and agile James Bond character, provided that the details of physical appearance are not continually stressed; similarly, many female Jane Austen devotees envisage Elizabeth Bennett as someone much like themselves.

So, we may take it as a working premise that a small amount of physical description of lead characters is probably required, in particular to assist your 'visual' readers to get the picture; but information about personality is paramount. Let us look at some possible techniques for this, with some example sentences of different kinds – intended only as instances, not as models of excellence – and then briefly examine how all of these might be combined to build a character throughout the narrative.

1. *The author can comment directly on a character.* At first sight this seems an obvious technique. The author simply tells the reader what he needs to know. Yet most successful modern writers do not spend paragraphs on descrip-

tion and personal information about their characters, especially not as an opening strategy. It may be that film and television have a role in this, the twenty-first-century reader is accustomed to seeing a character in action on the screen and deriving background information as he goes, in a way that previous generations were not. Beginning a novel nowadays by filling the reader in with all the background information on that check-list is an almost sure-fire way of ensuring that your manuscript will fail, even if authors of the past did things that way. It is still possible to give brief pieces of information directly, even in the first sentence, especially when description is linked to some activity:

> Peter Lewis walked along the road, a small, insignificant figure in a shabby overcoat.

Nonetheless, the important word is 'brief'. This is not the moment to launch into a paragraph of authorial comment about his background, hopes and fears. If you have a story to tell, get on with it. Small pieces of additional information can be fed in, in a similar way, throughout the narrative. However, there is an important exception here. Did you see Peter Lewis as black? Ten years old? From another century? Disabled? Any or all of those things might be true, but, if so, you must introduce that information early on. Remember that readers will bring their own assumptions with them, unless you tell them otherwise.

2. *The author can comment less directly,* by offering incidental description in the process of the narrative, while apparently concentrating on the person's actions. We have already seen a parallel technique for describing setting and it works equally well for characters.

> The doorbell! That would be the social worker now. Doris took a deep breath, straightened

her crumpled skirt and ran roughened fingers through her greying hair, before she went out into the hall to answer it.

Ask yourself how many facts you know about Doris as a result of that passage. Yet the story is not held up by the description.

3. *A character comments directly or indirectly on another.* This is a refinement on the previous technique and, when skilfully handled, can be extremely effective, since it removes the author's voice and appears to emerge from one of the characters instead. But it requires care to avoid producing terrible examples such as,

> Well, Lydia, tomorrow is the eighteenth birthday of our tall, red-headed daughter Sandra. Shall we invite her blue-eyed Irish boyfriend Tom to come to dinner here in our little thatched cottage in Somerset?

Yet many writers do what is essentially the same thing – make people tell each other things that they already know in order to convey that information to the reader. Yet, if you can avoid the pitfalls, this is a useful technique. If you can create realistic speech patterns (we shall look at ways of doing that later), you can tell the reader something about the speaker at the same time, and so sketch in information about two characters at once:

> It's all very well for her – all blonde hair and high heels and poshed up like something from a fashion catalogue. She hasn't got three squalling kids to bring up in a dump like this, with a fat slob of a husband who's always out of work.

4. *We learn what one character thinks about another.* The words do not have to be spoken necessarily. If you are using a 'viewpoint character' (*see* below) the description can be simply in the commentator's mind. This technique is particularly effective when used to describe personality rather than external facts, precisely because the speaker can be spiteful, blunt or even prejudiced in a way that an all-seeing author really cannot be. We see Heathcliff in *Wuthering Heights*, for example, as such a forceful character largely because we see him through biased Nellie's eyes.

5. *A character talks directly about himself/ herself.* This is an extremely useful strategem. It usually works best where your character has a friend, colleague or confidante to whom he (or she) can grumble about the past or confide personal hopes, doubts and plans. It can be used for background information, too –

> You know I've always had a fear of dark places.

And even, occasionally, for purely physical description:

> Yes, before you ask. I've had my hair cut, and dyed red. And I've bought this new black leather coat and jeans. Steve won't like it, but he'll have to lump it, won't he?

6. *A character thinks about himself.* More commonly physical description is given in the form of such inner thoughts, when the character is 'talking to himself'. A reflection, for instance, in a mirror, is often used as excuse for this. We see a character look at himself in the glass and discover, not only what he looks like, but what he thinks about it. Traditional romantic fiction often uses this:

> She looked at herself in the long mirror and noted with satisfaction that the green dress exactly matched the emerald of her eyes ....

It is particularly useful, of course, in the case of any character who is a little vain, or – conversely – one who lacks self-confidence.

However, this 'talking-to-oneself' technique becomes an invaluable tool when it is used to indicate the thinker's personality, rather than merely external appearance. Whether we 'see' a person thinking malicious thoughts, mentally planning brave deeds or being inwardly terrified, we derive a strong impression of his character.

7. *Through the character's own actions and attitudes.* The strongest way of demonstrating personality, however, is undoubtedly by showing how the character behaves and thinks. This is usually much more effective than any kind of direct description or comment by anyone. We believe that someone is kind-hearted if we see him doing something kind, cruel if we see him mistreat a person or an animal. What is more, we will probably continue to have that opinion whatever anyone else says in the course of the novel. This device can be deliberately used to enlist the reader's sympathy for someone who is misjudged (for good or ill) or in conflict with others in his environment. The reader then knows better than the other characters, which is always a strong position to create. Where thoughts and actions are in conflict, it creates a strong effect, and usually it is action which prevails. Someone who wishes bitterly to kick the cat, but then caresses it, is either secretly soft-hearted, or – if the caress is for an audience – comes across as strongly devious. In either case the conflict between thought and deed gives a forceful indication of inner character.

8. *Through the character's own general speech.* Speech is, of course, a kind of action and results from thought, so this is a specialized version of what went before. At the simplest level, a character who offers to do things for others will generally be perceived as kind, almost as surely as if he actually did them, and usually in rather fewer words. Also, some characteristics, such as spitefulness and tactlessness, are actually manifested in speech:

> What a pretty dress. Pity you couldn't find a bigger size.

But characters may say one thing and do another. This is akin to the thought–action conflict looked at earlier, and is another powerful way of demonstrating what a character is 'really like'. This is not always negative. Many adventure stories have a character who warns that the situation calls for the utmost care, but who then acts with reckless bravery – making his courage seem the greater by his words. Note, however, that the reader will invariably believe the deeds and not the words, demonstrating again the force of action as a way of creating personality. Another, more sophisticated way of showing personality is by paying attention not only to what a character might say, but to the whole way in which it is expressed, in particular to how he or she addresses other characters, and the way in which they are spoken to in return. We shall examine this in greater detail in Chapter 5 on dialogue.

9. *Through the way that other characters react.* This is another powerful device, when skilfully employed, and often affects the reader almost subconsciously. If a woman acts nervously when her husband is around, becomes unexpectedly clumsy for example, the reader will begin to draw conclusions about his nature even if nothing at all direct is said. If she speaks about him with affectionate disrespect, that will create a different 'personality' in our minds. Again, this method enables you to create two characters at once.

10. Finally, there are two quite random elements which, rather unreasonably, may influence how a reader perceives a character. The first of these is *names*. Names have been demonstrated to set up assumptions too, and,

no matter how irrational that is, it is helpful to the novel-writer to be aware of this. Some of these assumptions are based on a perception of what is fashionable at different times and among different groups. (How old is Kylie? Beatrice? Muriel? How rich is Michael? Fred? Tristan? What kind of school did Dwayne attend? Piers? Julian?) Sometimes there are overt reasons for all this; 'Phil', 'Nick' and 'Denny' are 'untrustworthy', for example, thanks to characters in soaps, whereas 'Will', thanks to the Prince, has recently become quite glamorous. Other widespread associations seem to have no rational cause at all and this is true even with 'neutral' names. An informal poll showed that 'Richard' was felt to conjure up someone 'upright and strong', 'Fred' someone older, practical and good-natured, but 'Robert' had rather negative associations. Interestingly, abbreviating the same name had a different effect: Bob and Robbie were seen as positive, whereas 'Dick' was definitely on the suspect list. Clearly, you cannot guess at every possible association of this kind, but it is a matter to pay attention to. If you are doubtful about what you have called a character, try a name-association game with your acquaintances. The results may surprise you, and in that way you can at least avoid calling your beautiful, twenty-year-old heroine by a name which conjures up maiden aunts to most of your readership. Remember also that it is not a good idea to have several characters with similar names, unless that is a requirement of the plot, since it difficult for the reader to remember who is who. The second of these random elements is *association with things that your characters possess*. This takes us back to the idea of setting – and to our original checklist too – and is largely a question of using the reader's general, and probably subconscious, assumptions. Casually mention that one of your young men drives a Porsche, owns a pit-bull terrier or has a model railway layout in the attic, and your reader is ready to assume a host of personality traits. Use this technique with caution, however, as it can lead to stereotypes. Did you for a moment assume that all three might be the same man? This device is notoriously much harder to manage when the setting is not modern Britain, because the reader may have no significant assumptions about other times and places. (What would be the equivalents in ancient Rome?)

APPLYING THESE TECHNIQUES IN NARRATIVE

Obviously, in the course of a novel these techniques will be combined. It is clearly impossible to give a full account of this, but here is an example of how this might be done. Suppose that we are writing a 'woman-in-jeopardy' thriller and want to build a lively heroine, we might begin like this:

The first hint of trouble came on Christmas Eve. Kylie jostled her way down the street, as quickly as her high-heeled boots and short leather skirt allowed. What had possessed her to wear those today? Only two hours left until the shops all closed; thank heaven the garage office where she worked had closed a bit earlier this afternoon.

She elbowed her way deftly past a fat woman with a brood of squalling kids, and ticked off the presents on her mental list. Chocolates for Gran, tools for brother Steve – he always had some old banger he was taking apart. Those were easy enough. But Dad? She couldn't give him a CD token yet again.

She glanced in the window of a big department store, hoping there was inspiration on display. And then she saw him: the same man as before. Big, tall, dark-skinned and menacing ...

These few paragraphs use a number of techniques. We have placed her on the street and in a crowd, in both of which she evidently feels at home. We have a passing reference to her clothes, which also helps to indicate her age, we know where she works and a certain amount about her family. There is an interesting omission here: she has a brother, a grandmother and a father, but no mention of a mother anywhere. Also, we have a tiny glimpse into her mind: these are not imaginative gifts, but she is thinking about other people, which makes her slightly sympathetic as a character. We also know that she does not plan ahead (last-minute presents and inappropriate clothes), thinks of herself as fairly slim, is dismissive of other people's children and is already nervous about this man. And we have her name.

The other character, the man who follows her, is introduced quite differently. There is a list of adjectives – we see him as Kylie does. Looking in the window-glass will give a further opportunity to sketch in her own appearance if we wish (cropped hair, nose stud and woolly fleece?) and her reaction to the man (making a weapon of the keys in her pocket?) will help us to understand her character.

A following scene in which she meets a friend would then enable her to voice her fears, and explain to us, as well as to the friend, where she has seen the man before and why he frightens her so much. We might also learn why Kylie cannot rely on her family for support (Dad is depressed and out of work, Steve is not interested, Gran is too old?); we may even discover where mother went. The friend's support and sympathy would make us feel more warmly to Kylie too, as well as understanding what her burdens are (she broke up with her boyfriend recently?). A scene with Gran might give another view: all the things that Gran is disapproving of, while Kylie shows herself as inwardly impatient, even rude, but

caring nonetheless, by helping an old woman who shows no gratitude. A tentative suggestion that she is at threat might be greeted with derision – what does she expect, the way she looks? – before Gran sends her out for cigarettes, into the streets where the man still lurks... And so on, throughout the book. The 'development' of Kylie's character might well be self-reliance and responsibility, both of which she has potential for.

WHOSE STORY IS IT, ANYWAY?

One very important consideration in creating character is the *viewpoint* of the 'narrator' – and that does not mean you, the author, necessarily.

1. *Eye-of-God.* You may decide to write the novel from an 'all-seeing author's' point of view: someone who knows all about everyone and everything in the story, because he or she created it all. That way you can see inside the minds of all the characters, you know the history of every building and the secrets of all the inhabitants. You can see why this is often referred to as 'eye-of-God' narration. However, this is a technique which requires great discipline. The very breadth of vision makes it easy to lose sight of whose story it is supposed to be, and lovingly to follow every character as if his or her motivation and point of view were of equal importance. This can be difficult for the reader, since (not being God) it is hard to identify with every character individually and fully empathize with each in turn. Ironically, the effect is often to create a degree of detachment from them all, so it is no longer a very popular technique. Many modern novels appear at first sight to make use of it but, in fact, if you read more closely, you will often find that the real viewpoint is one of the others outlined below.

2. Bystander viewpoint. This is a variation on the eye-of-God. Here all the actions and events are viewed dispassionately and nobody's private thoughts and motives are revealed except by what they individually do. These things are left for the reader to deduce. This is obviously a very detached way of telling a story and needs to be used for a particular effect, although it can be surprisingly effective in stories of great tragedy – think of *Schindler's Ark* – and is sometimes a successful way of writing comedy as well. The 'narrator' is almost an imaginary character, who takes no part in the action but, as it were, leans against a wall, watching.

3. Using a viewpoint character. Both of the above techniques use the third person for the narrative (that is, everyone in the story is 'he' or 'she'), and the reader is not invited to identify with any particular one; nowadays, however, simple third-person narrative is difficult to use successfully under the terms of the reader contract. There is another popular version of this technique, which is often much more effective. The story is told in the third person, but we are really seeing it through the eyes of one of the characters. We know his thoughts and attitudes and see the action as it unfolds to him. Compare the following examples. The 'bystander' narration would simply say:

'Hello, darling', he said. She frowned.

This can be told from her point of view:

'Hello, darling', he said. She frowned. She hated it when he called her 'darling' in that tone of voice. It always meant that he had something to hide.

Or from his:

'Hello, darling', he said, but she frowned back at him with her what-have-you-got-to-hide-now face.

4. Single viewpoint narrative. When there is only one viewpoint character, this is almost always the central one because the reader automatically identifies with the person whose thoughts and motives are revealed. However, second- or third-level viewpoint characters are possible for special purposes. The use of a single viewpoint imposes certain limitations on the author though, since obviously the character cannot know every-thing – other people's thoughts and motives, or things that happened when he was not there. In certain genres, detective novels for example, this can sometimes be an advantage since the author can quite reasonably keep some elements of the plot from the reader until the viewpoint character discovers them. Nevertheless, if an author chooses this tech-nique, he or she must be constantly aware of what the character can and cannot know or think.

5. Multiple viewpoint narrative. There is a more manageable variant on this, the so-called multiple viewpoint narrative. Here the view-point character can change, from chapter to chapter or even from scene to scene, thus allowing us to see the motives and thoughts of all the major characters in turn. This has all the advantages of the eye-of-God and yet encourages the reader to empathize. Indeed, precisely because we are inside the minds of several characters, the reader may often see conflicting interests from both points of view in a way that is not available by any other means. In a thriller, to know what is in the stalker's mind while also sharing the carefree thoughts of the threatened victim as she walks innocently towards her doom is a partic-ularly effective device for increasing tension.

However, it is important not to hop about between different viewpoints within a single scene, otherwise this advantage will be lost.

Obviously the multiple viewpoint brings problems of its own, to which consideration must be given. Each viewpoint character must have a distinctive view: thoughts, motives and emotions which relate to him alone and spring from his personality and circumstances. This means that all viewpoint characters must be fully rounded ones, although, as you will have deduced from what was said before, looking at things through their actions and reactions is often the easiest way of accomplishing this. One easy-to-achieve but effective technique is to describe events by using different imaginative strategies (as described in the previous chapter) for different characters. One viewpoint character will therefore describe chiefly action, space and feeling, another will tell you what he sees, a third perceive the world in terms of what he hears. A cognitive character who thinks exclusively in abstract, measured terms will automatically come across as cooler and detached – which may be useful for the plot.

Many authors take this further and give each viewpoint character a distinctive voice, meaning that vocabulary and sentence structure are subtly altered with each change of view. Often the reader is not aware of this, but it is extremely effective in making the story and the people 'real'. We shall examine techniques for doing this in the sections on dialogue and style.

Even so, the golden rule of using viewpoint characters remains: the character at any given time can only know what he or she can reasonably perceive. However, this is much less limiting with multiple, or, as we should perhaps call it, successive viewpoint narrative, since the constraints vary from scene to scene, and what one narrator does not know the next one might, and vice versa. Important events, unknown to your major character, can therefore be passed on to the reader by using a different character as a viewpoint for another scene.

One useful way to get the viewpoint right is to begin by writing any scene using a first-person narrative: That is, one of the characters becomes 'I'. Use the concrete visualization technique to 'see' the scene, as if you were the viewpoint character, and then write the scene from that point of view, including emotions, feelings and perceptions as well as what 'you' did. Then edit the manuscript, changing 'I' to 'he' or 'she'. With practice, this will become easier and you will be able to write the scene from within without going through the first-person narrative at all.

This exercise is a useful way of helping to ensure the rounded character that we mentioned earlier. A hero with no human weaknesses is not quite real (besides, it is difficult for the average reader to feel empathy with perfection), but if we can see inside his head we can discover that he is a little impatient, for example, though he may control this outwardly. Conversely, the most heartless

---

**Five-Minute Exercise:
Concrete Visualization**

Apply the visualization technique to a short scene from your novel. Choose an episode that involves two or more people, visualizing the scene from one character's point of view. Now repeat the exercise, taking the viewpoint of another character. How do the two versions vary in your mind? (They should!)

---

murderer will seem more real, not less, if he has some human sentiment: how many real-life murderers loved their mothers or their cats, or were taking revenge upon the world for some kind of rejection or rebuff? Seeing the world from their point of view can make the reader aware of this, without the need of a direct, 'eye-of-God' technique, although, of course, the villain will always see himself as justified.

However, be careful not to have too many viewpoint characters. Remember that the reader has to empathize, to some degree, with each viewpoint character. In a story of 50–60,000 words one or two are probably enough, though with novels in excess of 160,000 words obviously there is room for several more. Indeed, they may be required to give a novel of that length sufficient depth. Naturally there are exceptions, like Len Deighton's *Bomber*, where the point of the novel is that all the individuals have a life affected by the bombing raid, but such novels remain exceptional and require an artistic tour de force.

6. *First-Person Narrative.* It is, of course, possible to drop the pretence altogether (or, in fact, make the pretence more complete) and simply tell the story in the first person, where

one character becomes 'I'. This can be the main character or a lesser one, like Dr Watson or other detectives' partners, a technique we shall look at later. In either case, the writer must ensure that the personality of the narrator comes through, especially if the character is a central one. It is more than ever vital with this technique to see things from the character's own point of view: so if you want to show that the narrator is mean, he must not only be seen to act meanly but to pride himself on being sensibly careful as he does so. To have more than one 'I-narrator' is extremely difficult to do convincingly, although some stories have attempted it. The epistolary technique, based on an exchange of letters, is a variant of this, rather out of fashion nowadays.

7. *Stream of Consciousness.* This is sometimes called 'interior monologue' and is a specialized kind of first-person narrative, where we follow the narrator's thoughts and the effect of the events within the plot, rather than following these events themselves. In fact, the actual 'happenings' often have to be deduced by the reader, as the narrating character talks to himself, fantasizes about alternative realities and allows his thoughts to wander, as thoughts do. James Joyce and Virginia Woolf both experimented with this, and the best way to understand exactly how it works is probably to read James Joyce's *Ulysses.* It is an extremely difficult technique to carry off in its purest form, but most modern novels use a variant of it, in which real events are narrated by a viewpoint

---

Study Box

In these two contrasting passages, we can see how first-person narration can be effective in creating a character. Compare McDermid's feisty female detective with Murdoch's careful epicure, pedantically writing his 'memoir'.

If slugs could smile, they'd have no trouble finding jobs as car salesmen. Darryl Day proved that. Oozing false sincerity as shiny as a slime trail, he'd followed us round the showroom. From the start he'd made it clear that in his book, Richard was the one who counted. I was just the bimbo wife ...

Under normal circumstances, I'd have got a lot of pleasure out of telling him his tatty sexism had just cost him the commission on a twenty grand sale, but these circumstances were so far from normal, I was beginning to feel like Ground Control to Major Tom as far as

my brain was concerned. So instead, I smiled, patted Richard's arm and said sweetly, 'Nothing's too good for my Dick.' Richard twitched. I reckon he knew instinctively that one way or another, he was going to pay for this.

Val McDermid, *Crack Down*

It is after lunch and I shall now describe the house. For lunch, I may say, I ate and greatly enjoyed the following: anchovy paste on hot buttered toast, then baked beans and kidney beans with chopped celery, tomatoes, lemon juice and olive oil. (Really good olive oil is essential, the kind with a taste, I have brought a supply from London.) Green peppers would have been a happy addition, only the village shop (about two miles' pleasant walk) could not supply them.

Iris Murdoch, *The sea, the sea*

character, interspersed with paragraphs of thoughts and reactions in stream-of-consciousness as the character reacts to what is happening.

8. *Second-Person Narrative.* If there are third-person and first-person narratives, what about second-person? This would mean that the author was telling you 'your' story (not 'he did this' nor 'I did this', but 'you did this'). One or two authors have experimented with this idea, presupposing a car crash or a trial, but rarely with success: although Iain Banks's *Song of Stone* does use this technique. The result is usually contrived and, if one looks more closely, most are not true second-person narratives. The narrator is really another

character (if 'you' exist, 'I' must exist also). So the viewpoint of narration is really first-person after all.

CHECKPOINT 1

Think of a modern novel that you have recently read which uses a third person. Which of the above techniques does the author use? Is it really the 'eye-of-God', is there a single viewpoint character or more than one?

CHECKPOINT 2

What is the viewpoint of your novel or the one you plan? Who are the likely viewpoint characters?

As before, this exercise seeks to stimulate your imagination and at the same time integrate various of the techniques found in the preceding chapter. Note that this worksheet presupposes that you have worked through Worksheet One, so if you have not done so it is suggested that you go back and complete that before continuing, as what follows builds explicitly on that activity.

1. Once again, begin with a concrete visualization exercise. Return in your imagination to the place already visited in Worksheet One, beginning once more outside the building. As you move towards it, this time take the role of one of your lead characters – a viewpoint character if possible, but certainly a first-level one – who is associated in the story with that place.

Stand and look at the building once again, but now try to do so from the viewpoint of the character. What emotion does this place evoke – fear, pride, nostalgia, excitement, or simply proprietorial worries about rising damp? Walk towards it, noticing this time not your surroundings but your own identity. How do you move – quickly, slowly, doggedly, gracefully, with pain? Whatever the answer, try to be aware of it. Put out your hand as you go through the entrance and look at the hand – what does it look like? Is it old, young, beringed, or are the fingernails bitten to the quick? What shape are the fingers, and – as you take in your arm – what are you wearing? How do your garments feel around you as you move? What is on your feet? What do you look like? (Find somewhere to look at your reflection, if in doubt.)

2. Go through the entrance again and look around at all the things you established earlier. Ask yourself how tall you are, and see if that alters your perspective on the room. (You may realize that you mentally 'grow' or 'shrink' a inch or two, and have a rather different attitude.) Which objects in the room are you most familiar with? Which gives you any

sensation of pleasure or of pride? Which makes you most anxious or dissatisfied? Why?

3. Still in your adopted character, 'think back' to your last meal. Where was it? What did you eat? With whom? Try to visualize the scene – the sounds, smells and voices, and whatever you ate and drank your meal from. Did you enjoy it, hate it, or not think about it at all? What would you hate, refuse or particularly enjoy?

4. Based on the imaginary picture that you have, now try applying the 'personality questionnaire' to your chosen character:

a) Name, age, race and sex
b) Physical description
c) Job (what, where, how well paid, how do you get there?)
d) Important emotional ties (family, animals, friends, causes?)
e) Dress
f) Strengths and weaknesses
g) Likes and dislikes
h) Background (where born, educated?, and so on)
i) Habits and mannerisms
j) Home (where do you live?, what does it look like?, how well-maintained?)
k) What are your important possessions?

You may even ask yourself about the underwear. If you don't know now – find out!

5. Attempt to write a short scene (which may or may not be included in the novel) in which the character walks into the house, exactly as you have visualized. Do so, if possible, in first-person narrative – stay in the role of the character and write as 'I', but do not, for the moment, introduce any other people to the scene. If you have a similar incident in mind, in which a particular mood is evident, use that, re-running the picture in your mind and allowing that emotion to intrude.

4   MINOR CHARACTERS

Characters... are not caricatures of persons unknown to me, tributes to the author's friends and relatives or opportunities for settling old scores... They have strengths and failings, characteristic traits, and generally act from recognizable motives of some kind... The plot will not require me to believe in strange coincidences nor sudden changes of character, even if these have happened to the author in real life.

Reader contract

In a previous chapter we have considered some ways of creating major characters. What about the 'minor characters'?

SECOND-LEVEL CHARACTERS

Whatever their role in the unfolding of the storyline, the personality of these characters is important and their actions and motives matter to the plot. The author needs to know as much about these characters as the first-level ones, in order to make them psychologically consistent and have them leap up from the page, so that many of the techniques mentioned in the previous chapter will again apply. On the other hand, it is not always necessary to give all this information to the reader, especially not the first time that the character appears. It may be useful instead to decide what are the most salient characteristics and to make sure that these emerge early on, so that the reader has a strong impression of some kind and will recognize the character again. It can also be a good idea to give such individuals habits of speech, behaviour or dress which make them instantly identifiable. For this reason we may have to know more about the physical appearance of a secondary character than we know about a much more central one, but less about the nuances of personality, at least at first.

This physical description can be directly introduced (as with the stalker in the Kylie plot) by having a lead character as narrator – we thus see what the observer sees. The author may then disclose more and more of the secondary character's real nature as the story progresses, using the same techniques that we examined earlier, although this does not usually involve development as it would with a lead character. It is rather that characteristics which the reader has already glimpsed become more and more pronounced.

However, the reader will not feel cheated if, unlike with a viewpoint character, a second-level personality sometimes turns out not to be everything he or she appeared to be at first. Hence a secondary character may surprise the reader (and the central characters) by being an unexpected villain, living a secret life, possessing significant private information or simply having unsuspected traits, and this is obviously something an author can exploit without evoking a feeling that the 'contract' has been breached. This effect is most easily achieved if such secondary members of the

Five-Minute Exercise

Choose one of your second-level characters and work out a typical day's programme for that character, not as part of the story but as a character-rounding exercise. What, when not involved in furthering the plot, does he or she actually do? Be rigorous about this, start when the character wakes up and work out what fills up the hours of the day. (This is obviously a cognitive exercise.) Once you are familiar with the technique, apply it to your lead characters as well. This single exercise can do a great deal to combat woodenness and help to create a life beyond the page.

cast are introduced through the eyes of a lead character, whether the viewpoint character or not. As this character learns more and more about the truth of the other's personality, so the reader does too.

If defection or betrayal is involved, there is another powerful technique available. The truth can be disclosed through watching the turncoat character in action in scenes that do not at first involve the principals. A particular kind of anticipatory tension can be created in this way, since the reader knows more about the true personality than the hero or the heroine does, and is half-waiting for disillusion to occur, just as one agonizes for a friend who pins her hopes on someone unreliable.

Whether or not you include such scenes in which only secondary characters occur, you should have some idea of what these characters are doing in periods when they are not 'on stage'. They must have an imaginary life, even if the reader never learns of it in detail, thus avoiding impossibilities of time and place or one-dimensional characters who obligingly appear only when the storyline requires it. Nor are secondary characters an opportunity

to indulge in cameo sketches of real people whom the writer has encountered in real life. Naturally all your characters will share traits with actual people, otherwise they would have no life at all, but your life experience should simply provide you with a pool of potential attributes and appearances from which you can build the characters you need.

Your old school friend or that boss you grew to hate were not formed by your imaginary world and therefore they do not belong in it, however amusing that may seem to you. (It is astonishing how often a character that seems wholly improbable proves to be 'based exactly on my Aunty Kit'; this Aunty Kit, of course, was not a nineteenth-century mill-owner's wife, which may be why the transition does not work.) Remember the reader contract on this point, and make your characters compounds of the people you do know, or, better still, aspects of yourself, not cartoons or caricatures of individuals.

Above all, ensure that all your secondary characters have some function in the plot. Of course, they may give 'texture' to the novel, but it is not usually satisfactory to introduce a secondary character simply in order to achieve this end. The reader will quickly lose sympathy with a second-level character who is just there for ornament.

SOME TYPICAL FUNCTIONS FOR A SECONDARY CHARACTER

A secondary character often fulfils the role of assistant or confederate in some scheme or enterprise. Kylie's friend, in our imagined plot, was there for this reason. This enables the author to spell out the motives for and the drawbacks of the proposed action, as details are explained in dialogue. In adventure stories a complex plan of action is often expounded to the reader in the same way: it has to be spelt out to the confederate, who may then assist, achieve, betray or even bungle it. Secondary characters often trigger action too, directly or indirectly: Kylie's Gran may function in this role by sending Kylie into danger for her cigarettes. Most spy and adventure novels have someone who starts the central character on the quest: contemporary novels often have a secondary plot-line somewhere in the narrative; while almost every whodunnit has a range of second-level characters, several of whom are suspects for the crime.

Second-level roles may be triggers for emotion rather than for deeds. While a secondary character is not usually the subject of the central love affair in a romance, he or she may be the occasion for jealousy, hope, suspicion or despair. In a thriller there is often a subsidiary victim, who, being secondary, is expendable – a device which establishes additional terror for the central character who is under threat (Kylie's friend has borrowed Kylie's fleece and is discovered strangled in the street). In fact, any non-central character who creates significant conflict or tension, either emotional or actual, is probably best regarded as a second-level personality and rounded accordingly as a character.

Another subsidiary function of a second-level character, and one which we have touched upon elsewhere, is that of introducing and interpreting major characters when talking to other persons in the story. Clearly, the more we trust the secondary character, the more credence we will give to his evaluation of people and events. If we know him to be vindictive and unkind or biased and ill-informed, we shall approach his judgement accordingly. He may also give background 'factual' information, by gossiping or explaining things to other characters who are not in the know. However, the testimony of a secondary character may be unreliable, and this can provide the author with another useful strategy. Inaccurate or misleading facts given direct by the author are seen as a breach of the reader contract. But if an imaginary character gives such information (provided that there is a plausible reason for this) it will be regarded as an element of the plot. If any part of your storyline depends upon misunderstanding, misinformation or misinterpretation of the facts, it is worth considering the use of a secondary character to set this up for you.

The secondary character does not have to be malicious to achieve this effect. Your main character may draw an inference based reasonably on the testimony he has heard and act accordingly, although if he had personally witnessed the event he would have interpreted it quite differently, usually because the secondary character does not recognize some detail that is significant.

A secondary character may also be a viewpoint narrator for part of the story or for all of it. This can be a limitation or a plus factor. In *The Go-Between* (L.P. Hartley) the narrator was a child when the action took place and his innocence of the sexual relationship between the adults who used him as a messenger results in the story's having effectively two layers: the actual story of the ill-starred love affair, in which he is only a secondary factor, and the much more important emotional account of growing up – the experience of betrayal, exploitation and loss in which he is the central character.

CHECKPOINT 1

Look at the novel that you plan to write. Which are the secondary characters and what tension or action do they initiate? Jot down what you imagine to be the most salient characteristics of four of those characters. How can you divulge these to the reader and make the characters so memorable that the reader will recognize them again at once?

THE FUNCTION OF THIRD-LEVEL CHARACTERS

These, as we have said before, are characters who are still important to the action or the theme but who are not the primary participants. Often they occur quite briefly in the plot, being associated with a certain period or place and not appearing in the remainder of the story. Nonetheless, while they are on-stage, as it were, they may play a significant role in the mechanics of the plot, sometimes by acting as a catalyst, doing something, either deliberately or unwittingly, that triggers the subsequent events. They may create transient joy, unhappiness or tension, too, but not for the whole duration of the plot. They are not part of the final denouement, and this is what differentiates them from true second-level characters.

Another, alternative function of the third-level character is to be an *occasional* confidante and friend, allowing the main characters to share their thoughts. This is often an excellent way of presenting emotions, hopes and fears which people would not otherwise express, or of filling the reader in with background information. They do not initiate the action, although they may give significant advice or even act as co-conspirators, although only on the initiative of a major character, and they do not usually influence the outcome very much. (This is not confined to novels, of course. The nurse in *Romeo and Juliet* occupies exactly this sort of role.)

Sometimes the third-level character may exist chiefly as a link between different periods or places or to carry on the theme (which we shall examine later), usually by allowing the main characters to exhibit their characteristics or by providing a strong contrast to these traits. In this role a third-level character may even be a viewpoint narrator, especially where the author wishes to withhold some germane information from the readership. Detective fiction is an obvious example here. The function of Captain Hastings in Agatha Christie's Poirot books is not only to provide a willing sycophant, ready to marvel at his patron's skill. The fact that he does not always understand is crucial to his function as narrator: he cannot tell the reader what he does not know and so the author is excused from divulging everything.

This raises the question of the sidekick role, in particular. It is a specialized form of confidante and has advantages, although it is less commonly used nowadays. A degree of stupidity in the narrator is no bad thing, 'A little less intelligent than the readership', one commentator said. Many modern police novels achieve a similar effect by avoiding such a viewpoint character but by having instead sleuths who work in pairs. This means that the lead character does not have to know everything at any given moment in the plot. Sometimes the two sleuths do not get on, so one – usually the lower-level character – can actually mislead the other, and the reader, or keep important information back. Often the sidekick is a third-level character, at other times a second-level one. Dr Watson, in the Sherlock Holmes adventures, is an interesting case: a secondary character in the early stories, he becomes almost third-level in some later ones.

SKETCHING THIRD-LEVEL CHARACTERS

Whatever the role, even these third-level characters must have some individuality, a physical appearance, strengths and weaknesses. We do not need to know them inside out, but we must understand in general terms what makes them tick. Since they give flavour to the story, it is particularly important that they behave, dress and speak in ways that are consistent with the time and place in which the narrative is set.

However, it is a common error to write too much description of such characters. A good rule of thumb is that the author should know twice as much about them as is written on the page, that they should have one or two defining characteristics and should behave predictably throughout.

E.M. Forster, that great novelist, in *Aspects of the Novel*, identifies these characters as legitimately 'flat' and notes their function for the novelist:

> They are easily recognized when they come in... [and] are very useful to the author since they never need reintroducing, never run away, need not be watched for development and provide their own atmosphere.

These characters are rather like the people we come across incidentally in daily life: we gain a general impression, which may be slightly strengthened or modified by later meetings, but essentially we do not know them well enough to change that first impression much. In novels, what matters to the reader is how these characters are perceived by the first-level characters, and that is probably the best way of presenting them, although of course, if you are writing as eye-of-God or a bystander you will have to find a different technique.

Create your third-level characters by giving them broad characteristics, a strong physical presence and distinctive speech. They may have individual possessions, habits, clothes or names, but not all of these. Once you have established them, however, it is sufficient to refer to what the reader knows. No further character development is generally necessary nor desirable and these characters should be relied upon to act and speak in fairly predictable ways. Indeed, as that quotation from Forster says, their very predictability is part of their value to the novelist. Such characters give texture and atmosphere and are often necessary to the plot, but a few well-drawn ones are better than a multitude. In fact, the more third-level characters you introduce, the more difficult it is for the reader to remember all of them and the more skill the narrative requires.

CHECKPOINT 2

Do you envisage any third-level characters in the novel that you plan? (Often they emerge as you are writing and your imaginary world becomes more real to you; if so, delay this exercise until it is appropriate or apply it to a novel you have read.) What are their salient characteristics, either physical or behavioural, which will help the reader to remember them? Are there any constraints of background, time or place which will affect the way they think and act?

FOURTH-LEVEL CHARACTERS

Fourth-level characters exist, as we have seen, chiefly because of what they do. Sometimes they have important roles to play because of that function – that cab-driver, for instance, following the heist – but what makes them 'fourth-level' is that any person in that role would do. It does not matter whether the cabbie is black or white, or whether he has hair or not, the important thing is that he drives a cab and does or does not catch up with his prey. The individual's personality is unimportant here.

It can be amusing to create a cameo and have a garrulous, bald-headed cynic with a tattooed arm, but that is not vital to the story-line. In general, it is probably a better idea to avoid lavishing description on fourth-level characters and to concentrate on a single attribute: he is bald-headed *or* tattooed *or* garrulous. This is enough to create the impression of vivid liveliness, without requiring the reader to hold in mind another complex character who does not affect the plot. We have already noted that fourth-level characters do not require names.

Just occasionally a fourth-level character may be the means of passing on some information which is vital to the plot. For example, the waiter who tells the hero, 'The gentleman has just left, sir.' However, treat this device with caution and save it for occasions when the information derives direct from the role, thus the waiter might notice what the villain ate, but beware of basing the plot on what he happened to overhear. This may occur in real life, but is inclined to seem contrived in fiction, unless of course, somebody has paid this particular waiter to listen in. If he has some motive of his own, he should not be fourth-level anyway.

All this means that fourth-level characters are almost never used as narrators, since the very act of telling the story gives the character a personality which lifts him to a higher-level role. There are a few exceptions here, of course. Where multiple viewpoint is employed, a fourth-level character is occasionally called upon to explain to some authority what he saw, generally because all the central characters are dead, and his role as an outsider at the end gives the narrative a certain poignancy. But do not confuse this with the viewpoint narrator of Daphne Du Maurier's *Rebecca*, for instance, who has no name but obviously does not fall into this class. The second Mrs De Winter is a first-level character and the suppression of her name is a deliberate device, reinforcing the narrator's view of herself as insignificant compared with Rebecca, who is named throughout.

CHOOSING NAMES FOR MINOR CHARACTERS

On the subject of names, a final word: try not to choose names for second-, third- and fourth-level characters which are too similar to each other or to those of your higher-level ones. Even names beginning with the same letter may be confusing, unless that is an element of plot. The reader will soon forget who is 'Des' and who is 'Dan'. If two names are rather similar call the lower-level character some other name instead. Some people find this difficult because they are attuned to the name they have already used; in this case choosing another name with the same syllabic rhythm may make it easier (for example, 'Oliver' becomes 'Timothy' rather than 'James'). If the same first letter is inevitable, because two characters need the same initials, for example, it may help to choose two names of different length or which otherwise have a different shape on the page: 'Jemma' and 'Jenny' are easily confused, 'Joy' and 'Jennifer' are much more distinct.

KEEPING YOUR CHARACTERS CONSISTENT THROUGH THE PLOT

There are authors, including some famous ones, who like to keep a card-index of the minor characters, noting down the details of each: appearance, dress and the most important traits of character. This avoids the situation where the blue-eyed friend who turns up on p.2 develops hazel eyes a little later on, and, if your imaginative strategies are chiefly cognitive, this technique may well work for you (*see* Chapter 2 for how to discover your imaginative style).

However, do ensure that, if you choose this method, you begin by envisaging the character, for instance through a visualization exercise, and then make a note of what you 'see'. To decide on the characteristics first and then create a character to fit, too easily leads to one-dimensional results. Your surly farmer

---

Study Box

Look at the following passages to see how minor characters are used for different purposes. The first is taken from the beginning of a novel, where a (nameless) fourth-level character gives his captain – and therefore the reader – information that is essential to what follows: the puzzling disappearance of the ship and all aboard her. (In this whole introductory chapter only Dupree is named – given what you now know about the plot, why do you think this is?)

> A buzzer sounded and the officer on watch, a tall raven-haired lieutenant, picked up the bridge phone. Unseen by the voice on the other end, he nodded twice and hung up.
>
> 'Control room,' he said, briefly. 'Echo sounder reports the sea floor has risen fifteen hundred feet in the last five miles.'
>
> Dupree turned slowly, thoughtfully. 'Probably a small range of underwater mountains. We still have a mile of water beneath our keel.' He grinned and added. 'No worry about running aground.'
>
> The Lieutenant grinned back. 'Nothing like a few feet for insurance.'
>
> Clive Cussler, *Pacific Vortex*

The next example is taken from the end of a story, where the hero returns home victorious, but wounded and ill. This could have presented a problem for the author, since Bolitho is effectively a viewpoint character (another example of 'apparent' third-person form) and a direct account of his return might have made him seem mawkish or self-pitying. The author overcomes this by glossing over actual events and allowing him to focus instead on 'blurred memories' of minor characters, a device which also allows us to see the affection in which our hero is held by one and all. (Note that Allday has already been described in the previous paragraph as 'ever at his side'.)

> Again pictures in his mind were blurred and painful. Of his married sister, Nancy, organising his reception in the old grey house below Pendennis castle, being very brave and hiding her dismay at his gaunt appearance and inability to speak more than a few words to her. Of Mrs Ferguson, his housekeeper, red-eyed and fussing over him between bouts of weeping. Of Ferguson, his one-armed steward, helping Allday to settle him in ... bed.
>
> Alexander Kent, *Passage to Mutiny*

---

should be a man who is surly, not a personification of surliness and little else.

If you have a strongly visual imagination, creating consistent mental pictures may be easier for you, but to make a note of appearance and the salient characteristics of your characters is still a good discipline, especially in your earliest attempts. If you have an artistic aptitude, a quick pencil sketch may help to fix details in the mind. Audial thinkers may find it helpful to try to conjure up a quality of voice, perhaps by reading dialogue aloud, while those of a kinaesthetic bent may find a typical gait or gesture helps to give a minor character differentiated life. (I know one author who, when writing, often twists her face into a scowl or a smile, depending on which character is on the page).

Whatever method you choose, do try to ensure that your minor characters have individuality and consistency, for you as well as for your readers.

Five-Minute Exercise: Which Level Character?

This takes the form of a questionnaire. Take a familiar children's story, such as Cinderella, and work out the following (try to apply it to the story and not the pantomime, which conforms to different traditions):

1. Who is the lead character or is there more than one? Is her appearance, role or character the most vital to the plot?
2. Who is the viewpoint character or is there more than one?
3. If there is more than one, why and when does the viewpoint change? (Usually it is because the lead character is not there for an important scene; is that the case in your example too?)
4. Who are the secondary characters? Is personality and appearance more or less important here? If these characters have names (in a nursery story they may not), are they memorable and different?
5. Are there any third-level characters? If so, what is the salient characteristic of each?
6. Any fourth-level characters? (Think of footmen, pages or messengers.)

Obviously, a nursery tale like this is much simpler than a novel such as yours. The characterization is not drawn from life and is greatly oversimplified, so many of the foregoing techniques do not apply. However, the exercise will serve to indicate the principle of differing levels of character. Some of the answers may surprise you, too.

Worksheet Three – Minor Characters

Again, this worksheet is based on previous material, so if you have not completed previous worksheets it is strongly recommended that you do so before continuing, as decisions made as part of those activities are a prerequisite for what follows here.

1. Begin with a writing exercise this time. Rewrite the previous incident in first-person narrative – stay in the role of the character and write as 'I' (but do not, for the moment, introduce any other people to the scene).

2. Next, think of another character connected with the same locality, and whom your viewpoint character will meet, and slightly know – but who is not another first-level character. Where, in the building you have chosen, will they meet? (Use your cognitive strategies here.) Once you have decided this, resume the visualization process and go with your character to the meeting-point, deciding at the same time what brings your viewpoint person there. (Exploring? Looking for someone else? Going to the lavatory? Just part of ordinary daily routine? Simply relaxing in a chair?) Now 'see' the other person through your character's eyes – what kind of an impression do you have? Allow your character secretly to view the other person with any inner prejudices that you know they have, even if these are not outwardly expressed.

3. Write a brief (no more than twenty words) thumbnail sketch – using your viewpoint character's words and not your own – describing this other person to a friend. Then apply the questionnaire again, asking yourself which questions your viewpoint character would know the answers to, and which would

only be a kind of guess.

a) Name, age, race and sex
b) Physical description
c) Job (what, where, how well paid, how do you get there?)
d) Important emotional ties (family, animals, friends, causes?)
e) Dress
f) Strengths and weaknesses
g) Likes and dislikes
h) Background (where born, educated, and so on)
i) Habits and mannerisms
j) Home (where do you live?, what does it look like?, how well-maintained?)
k) What are your important possessions?

It should be clear to you at once that – as has been pointed out in the course of the text – not all of the questions are appropriate, and that appearances are far more important for a lesser character than for a major one, where other things are more significant.

Would it occur to your viewpoint character to hazard a guess about the underwear? If so, who does that tell us more about, the viewpoint character or the other one?

4. You might now wish to note down on a card details about the lower-level character, including your narrator's attitude. Don't write anything your viewpoint character did not 'say'. The card can be added to later – although not changed – if another viewpoint character describes that person too. This may modify the reader's view, as different people notice different things, but will generally tell us more about the people observing than about the one being observed.

5   DIALOGUE

Characters will speak as I recognize that people might genuinely speak in the situations arising in the plot, and there will be slight individual differences so that I can tell major characters apart. They will not all speak in exactly the same way, nor exactly as the author does.

Reader contract

WHAT IS DIALOGUE?

Most of us have some idea what dialogue in a novel is. We might offer some definition such as, 'when the characters speak to one another, and we read their actual words'. Normally, we recognize it on the page, because it is usually broken up into shortish paragraphs and marked by inverted commas or speech marks. It is also, as we have seen, an important way of showing character.

Authors are often advised to make dialogue as 'realistic' as possible, by listening to people in the street, but this is actually rather a simplified view. Writing successful dialogue is far more than simply transcribing conversation. In fact, dialogue in a novel is not really conversation in the normal sense at all. Consider this exchange, transcribed, more or less verbatim from real life:

> 'Hello, Joan.'
> 'Morning, Tom. How are you?'
> 'Fine. And yourself?'
> 'Fine. Lovely weather we've been having.'
> Yes, lovely.'

This may be conversation, it may even be authentic, but that does not mean that it is useful in your narrative. The first and most important rule of dialogue is that everything your characters say must have a function in the story. It may give us information, help to define the character or establish motive, mood or a state of mind.

HOW DIALOGUE DIFFERS FROM CONVERSATION AND FROM CONNECTING PROSE

Look at the above exchange again. Apart from telling us the names of the speakers, it does not furnish us with any significant information. It does not even tell us much about the speakers, beyond the fact that they are friendly and of a certain age. If such a casual exchange did appear in a novel, it would probably assume an importance that it did not have in reality, suggesting that good weather had some particular significance for the events that follow. This should alert us to the truth, that dialogue in a novel is a tool. It does not even follow the forms of real-life conversation on the whole. Listen carefully to people talking next time you are in a bus, a shop or any other public place: it may surprise you to find that genuine conversation between friends is so apparently unstructured. People begin sentences and do not finish them grammatically. Their speech is peppered with noises such as 'um' and 'er'.

Often they say the same things in different ways, or finish an explanation with an expression such as 'you know'. This is because spoken English has its own rules and conventions, distinct from those which govern written prose. We abandon sentences if we can see that our audience already understands or has lost interest, or repeat them if we feel that a point has not been taken. We make noises to demonstrate that we are in the middle of a sentence and do not want to be interrupted and we use gesture instead of an accurate vocabulary.

There is nothing wrong in any of this; in fact, if people do not talk like this, it is often difficult to hold a conversation with them. Yet it is difficult to capture on the page, because so much depends upon the tone of voice. Written English generally requires more a formal construction, because we cannot hear nor see the person speaking and are therefore totally reliant on the words alone. On the other hand, dialogue is not connected prose either. Since it pretends to be conversation, many of the conventions of spoken English are essential. Words and even sentences are shortened and idiomatic expressions appear. 'I shall not come to your house until after I have briefly visited my father' is a perfectly sensible sentence, but not one which a character is likely to say in informal, modern English, even in a book. Some would-be authors have difficulty with this, believing that to write, 'I won't be round till I've popped in to Dad' is somehow undesirable, and that 'I didn't ought to leave him on his own' is impossible and wrong, whoever the speaker is supposed to be. In order to understand why this is not the case, it might be helpful to examine briefly an area of linguistics known as 'register'.

WHAT IS REGISTER?

Register is the technical term for the degree of formality in language and the vocabulary and sentence structure used. All of us have an individual register, depending on our background, age and education. Real people often have little tricks of speech, phrases and colloquialisms which they frequently use, and to give such habits to your characters will make them seem much more authentic, although it is important not to overdo this. Do not be afraid to let characters speak in slightly ungrammatical or even clichéd ways, if that is appropriate to the character. If the people in your story are younger than you are yourself, and are contemporary, ensure that they do have a 'modern' feel and do not speak exactly as you used to do. Actual slang dates quickly, however, so use it sparingly.

Another area which requires care is the use of dialect. Perhaps it is important that your character is a Scot, for example, but resist the temptation to make him say things such as 'Och aye the noo.' It will either appear comic or hold up the flow of the narrative while the reader battles with paragraphs of non-standard English. Once again, a hint or two is best. An odd 'aye' or 'och', if you must, interspersed throughout the dialogue will remind the reader to 'listen' for a Scottish accent. There is an adage that written dialect alienates two kinds of reader: those who speak like that and those who do not.

However, these personal differences apart, all of us alter the kind of language that we choose depending on circumstance; indeed, the ability to do this appropriately is a mark of linguistic competence. The same message may be conveyed with varying degrees of formality depending upon who the speaker is, who is spoken to and what the topic and social circumstances of the conversation are. Naturally, this is important for the novelist, although not all registers can be reproduced in dialogue. For our purposes we may think of four separate ones: intimate, relaxed, informal

---

**Observation Exercise –
Capturing Intimate Register**

Next time you are in a public café or restaurant, look at the body language between other groups. Who leans forward towards whom? Who turns away? Who laughs, who smiles, who keeps aloof? These are elements that you can try to recreate, because the visual signals are actually part of the conversation that is happening. You can use concrete visualization to help you here. Close your eyes and try to look back to the last exchange you had with a close friend or intimate. Where did it take place? What were you wearing, and what did you talk about? Recreate the scene as fully as possible. Think about the body language that was used: apart from any overtly sexual content, which you may not want to use in your writing, what gestures or expressions were used?

---

and formal (further reading on this topic is suggested in the bibliography).

Intimate Register

This is reserved in real life for intimates and close friends and depends heavily upon the shared information and background of the participants. To an outsider, the words may not make any sense at all. There is typically little grammatical structure, few, if any, complete sentences, hardly any precise vocabulary and little information is exchanged. This is because the words are much less important than the tone of voice, the intonation and the body language which accompany them, and that is why it is almost impossible to recreate this on the page. Probably the best technique for suggesting this register to the reader is not to attempt to transcribe the actual words, but

to indicate the body language which accompanies them. Someone looking into someone else's eyes, to take the most obvious example, is a strong sign to the reader that the relationship is close even if the actual dialogue that you write has to be in a non-intimate register.

Relaxed Register

This is the register which one hears often on the bus, when people who know each other exchange news or gossip when they meet. In it, real information can be exchanged, though sentences are often not grammatically complete ('Love your hat', rather than 'I love your hat'); there are lots of contractions such as 'don't' and deliberately idiomatic 'softeners' such as 'kind of' or 'you know'. Facts and opinions are often repeated several times, and there is little technical vocabulary. A carburettor will become a 'carb', or a vacuum vortex a 'dust-whirlie thing'. Much of the conversation is a social mechanism, no more, in which one party tells another something he already knows, simply in order to allow him to agree.

If you have ever met anyone who does not 'play' according to these rules and who wishes to discuss the topic in more depth (the weather, for instance, in that first exchange above), you will recognize that this person may have problems in sustaining casual relationships and may even be regarded as 'difficult'. This is because dealing with detailed information is not appropriate to this register. But if you want to create a difficult character this may be a useful attribute to ascribe to him:

'Nice weather we've been having.'
'Think so? Seems bloody cold to me. And there's another wet front coming in.'

In a novel there is rarely room for much of this (unless you want it for a special effect, like that above) as it often appears rambling and meaningless. To create the impression that your characters are talking in this relaxed way, it is enough to hint at the conventions occasionally – using pet names and missing out the initial words of sentences, for example. Incorrect grammar, meaningless questions, slang and the use of strong language can also be features ('Me? Aren't bloody going, am I?'). It is probably a good idea to avoid the repetition element, however, since this is tedious when written down, unless you want to create a tedious character, of course.

Informal Register

This is the register that is chiefly used in speech to pass on complex information or to interact with people whom we do not know well. Sentences are generally complete, though not always wholly grammatical, and have sub-clauses, starting with 'which', 'when' or 'because'. Technical vocabulary occurs, though it may be immediately explained, and words such as 'cannot' may appear instead of 'can't', depending on just how formal the situation is.

Two-word verbs ('call on', 'ring up') may be avoided in favour of single-word expressions ('visit', 'telephone'), anecdotes are told in the past tense (not 'This girl comes up to me and she says...', but 'A young woman came up to me and said...'), and there are far more adjectives and adverbs generally. The degree to which this happens indicates how formal the situation is perceived to be. This is a register that can be written down, because it does not depend on the tone of voice so much, and most dialogue is written in this form. This means that the author is operating within a more limited range than 'real conversation' and so must take especial care over subtle alterations in things such as contractions, length of sentences and vocabulary to indicate greater informality where it is appropriate.

Formal Register

This is the highest register in which unrehearsed speech can occur. The content and general structure of each sentence is decided before utterance begins and therefore grammatical structure is usually complete. Vocabulary is carefully chosen and often complex, sentences and paragraphs are long with many sub-clauses. There are no contractions, idioms nor slang, although there may be set phrases – think of votes of thanks or parliamentary debates – and use is often made of the 'passive voice', for example, one might say 'it is often thought' rather than 'people think'. Some aspiring authors, recognizing this register as the one in which we most usually write, attempt to use it for their dialogue, supposing it to be 'correct'. This has the effect of making characters seem unnaturally stilted and formal. We sometimes describe a person as 'talking like a book', and that description is very apt – he is speaking in a 'written' register. If you wish to have a character who appears pompous and remote, of course, making him speak in this way will help. However, for the most part the trick is to make the dialogue appear to be natural conversation, although in fact it is nothing of the kind. Understanding register will help you in this task, although most readers are not aware of it, only of the results that it achieves.

The Effects of Using the Wrong Register

The effect of using too low a register for a given situation suggests a lack of education or social skill in the speaker. This is perhaps why, when some friends or lovers argue, rather than resorting to incoherent roars, they become more formal in their speech (sometimes continuing to say 'darling' all the while); this both removes the intimacy and puts the other party – still operating in a lower register – at a disadvantage. Using a higher register than is appropriate, as we have seen, makes the speaker seem cold, remote and intellectual. Once you understand the principle, you can exploit all this in your dialogue.

Historical Registers

This analysis clearly applies to modern speech. Whether it applied 200 years ago we cannot tell, since there was no way of recording spoken words, although it does appear that there has been a consistent trend towards more informal spoken registers as time goes by. This was once a mark of lack of education, but this is emphatically no longer true, perhaps as education has ceased to be confined to the elite. This is an issue if you are writing historic dialogue, since it raises the problem of how to make your characters seem realistically of the period, without at the same time making them appear boring, pompous and remote. Look at Jane Austen's characters for an indication of how upper-middle-class people addressed each other, at least in public, in Napoleonic times.

Nevertheless, this alteration is a real event. 'It is I' may be grammatically correct, but few people say it any more. The only solution appears to be the choice of a register only a little higher than would be current now, and introducing one or two features of more formal speech, simply to give a flavour of an old-fashioned style.

Conversely, there is a current trend towards using the markers of relaxed register – 'sort of', 'like', 'y'know' – in situations such as radio interviews, where this would not have been generally acceptable even a decade or two ago. This means that older people may conform to different norms and use a more formal register than younger ones, especially in a semi-formal atmosphere. Ensure that, if you are writing modern dialogue, you take account of this.

CHECKPOINT 1

Look at a section of dialogue that you have written. In which register does it chiefly fall? Is this appropriate to your characters and to the situation they are in?

USING DIALOGUE TO GIVE BACKGROUND INFORMATION

It has already been said that dialogue can be used to give information about characters. If someone says, 'What lovely curly hair Tom's got,' we do not need that physical description again. We have also already looked at the role of the 'confidante' who allows the chief character to discuss hopes, fears, plans and past events in a realistic fashion, freeing the author from the necessity of writing overt passages of narrative background which interrupt the story.

However, there are techniques for giving information which are far less obvious than this. A writer can imply, in a snatch of dialogue, a wealth of information that he would otherwise have to spell out to the reader:

'How are we this morning, Mr Prowse?'
'Feeling a bit better, thank you, nurse.'

This may not be earth-shattering dialogue, but it tells the reader a great deal. We know that one of the characters is called Prowse (dialogue is an excellent way of establishing names) and the other is a nurse. It is morning, and Mr Prowse has not been well. Also, unless we discover otherwise, we shall probably assume that Prowse is no longer young and that the nurse is fairly brisk and businesslike. That is a lot of information to convey in just two lines. And what do you suppose the setting is? Authors often begin a novel with a line of dialogue that points to a location in that kind of way. Furthermore, as an understanding of register will tell us, dialogue can suggest information about the speaker, because the vocabulary and sentence structure tell us, or should tell us, what kind of person that speaker is.

Look at this example. George Parker has been away for three weeks, and no one knows where he has been. When he gets back he meets five people: his wife, his boss, his cleaning lady, his mistress and his best friend. From the following lines of dialogue, which do you suppose is which?

> 'Morning, Parker. Haven't seen you for a bit. No problems, I trust?'
>
> 'George, where the hell have you been?'
>
> 'Why, it's Mr Parker! Haven't seen you for ever such a long time. I was only saying to my Kenny this morning, I haven't seen that Mr Parker in ever such a long time.'
>
> 'Morning, George. Long time, no see. What have you been up to, you jammy bastard?'
>
> 'Why did Georgie-Porgie leave little Miss Muffett all on her lonesome then?'

These decisions should not be difficult, but now think back and ask yourself whether you have any kind of picture of the speakers here. How old is the boss, for example? What is he wearing? Any impressions about how he might look? Try the same thing on the other characters. Most importantly of all, what gives you this impression? (This is an interesting exercise to try on a group, the amount of agreement might astonish you.) Of course, these people do not exist at all, they are only lines of dialogue, but they reveal much about what each speaker is like. When you write a line of dialogue, ask yourself, is this speech creating the right picture in the reader's mind?

If you have chosen a first-person narrative or stream of consciousness technique for your

---

Five-Minute Exercise

A woman goes to the door of a house looking for an old friend. The door is opened by somebody she does not know, who agrees that the friend lives in the house but is not there at present, and the visitor is invited in. A completely neutral form of this might be: 'She's not here at the moment. Come in.'

Rewrite that line of dialogue as it might be spoken by:

1. An elderly, dithery grandmother.
2. A surly, suspicious husband.
3. A fluffy-headed friend.
4. Anyone of your own characters that you choose, taking into consideration time and place (a Georgian aristocrat would not be answering his own door, for example).

---

novel, remember that this pretends to be the voice of the character. That makes it a kind of specialized dialogue. It, too, must match the speaker.

OTHER WAYS OF SHOWING PERSONALITY THROUGH DIALOGUE

There is another kind of information that dialogue conveys. It is much more subtle and it cannot be relied on as a narrative device, but it is a potent way of giving added reality to your central characters. Dialogue suggests a great deal, not only about the person speaking, but also about the person being spoken to. Think back to the example that we worked through just now. How old is George Parker, do you think? What is his job? What does he wear to work? What kind of house does he live in? The chances are that you do have some kind of answer to these questions, based entirely on the register of other people's dialogue. Even if you have no actual picture there are almost certainly things that you are no longer prepared to believe about him. (Is he a seventeen-year-old motor mechanic with a pierced tongue, living in a caravan?) As a novelist, you should have picked up at least that his best friend's idiom dates him as in his late forties or fifties, his boss's register suggests formality and his mistress tries so hard that she cannot be young any more.

In real life we are adept at deriving this kind of information about people, simply from the way other people talk to and about them. In a novel you cannot rely entirely on such subtle cues – a reader is interested in the plot, not psychological detective work – but the ability to create them is a useful skill. Conversely, a good story can easily be spoiled because those

---

Study Box

In these two extracts, two very different authors use speech patterns to help delineate a character. In the Vincenzi, the two young people have just met at a ball and the male character is permitted to achieve ascendancy at once. The heroine repeats herself, asks meaningless questions and utters incomplete sentences, while he effortlessly uses a higher register. Note the body-language, too.

'No,' she said, 'Of course not, nothing at all, I just thought I should –'

'Should what?' he said, his eyes moving over her slowly and deliberately as if studying some interesting object that he had found. 'If you want to sit down, we could go into the small bar over there. It's very hot in here. You do feel rather – warm.'

'Do I?' she said, stupidly, and 'Yes' he said, his eyes very serious. 'Really extremely – warm.' And indeed she did, very warm, almost feverish. 'So let's go and have a drink of something cool. And talk for a while.'

'I really ought to –' she said, and stopped again.

Penny Vincenzi, *Something Dangerous*

In the second extract, although of a completely different time, register is again the key. A lady of no great intellect condemns herself by the inappropriate subject matter and manner of her speech. We will not be surprised, when the moment comes, to learn that her judgement is unreliable.

'You've seen Mrs Thorpe, then?'

'Yes; I went to the Pump Room as soon as you were gone and there I met her, and we had a great deal of talk together. She says there was hardly any veal to be got at market this morning, it is so uncommonly scarce.'

'Did you see anybody else of our acquaintance?'

'Yes; we agreed to take a turn in the Crescent. We met Mrs Hughes and Mr and Miss Tilney walking with her ... Miss Tilney was in a very pretty spotted muslin, and I fancy, from what I can learn, that she always dresses very handsomely.'

Jane Austen, *Northanger Abbey*

hidden signals are working against your narrative. Readers will not warm to your hero if everyone around him treats him with cautious courtesy: they will pick up, without even realizing it, the information that this man is a little difficult. Make people speak to him in a more relaxed register and readers will see him as approachable, again without consciously recognizing why.

DIALOGUE AS ACTION – ADDING PACE

It is often said that dialogue adds pace to a novel and most of us are aware that this is true. Partly this is a result of the conventions of printing. A long, uninterrupted passage of narrative or description creates a solid block of printing on the page. Dialogue breaks up these blocks. You can use a line or two of speech, even a character speaking to himself, deliberately to achieve this effect. However, the same thing is also true in reverse. If you find yourself with a page or two of unbroken dialogue, it is a good idea to add an occasional line of action in between. This may be as simple as, 'he put down his cup', but it serves to return the reader to the scene.

Dialogue is a form of action, too, and if it is convincing it always speeds the pace. The characters themselves are speaking, and that gives the impression that the words are more immediate and 'real' than what is in the linking passages. (In fact, the opposite is true: the author is telling his imaginary story through the imaginary character. All the same, if a character says, 'Isn't he good-looking?', the reader will believe the character more than the author.) In addition, the rhythm of spoken English is different, especially in informal registers. Sentences tend to be shorter and so do paragraphs, and a change of rhythm also alters pace. We shall look at these aspects again more fully later.

Five-Minute Exercise: Background Information through Dialogue

Choose a character (preferably from your novel, but any character you have ever created will do). Make a note of four important facts about that character: for example, background, job, whether married, personality traits, appearance, weaknesses or dress, whatever is important to the character.

1. Set up a dialogue between that character and someone else in which your chosen facts emerge or can be easily deduced. Try to choose an appropriate register for each speaker in the exchange. Do not, for the purposes of the exercise, use direct questions such as, 'What's your name?' In an appropriate setting in the novel, a tense interrogation scene, for instance, such questions can obviously be used, but the object of this exercise is something else.

2. Now try to write a realistic dialogue between two other people, in which the same four facts emerge.

Which did you find easier, and why?

Some writing courses lay down rules and suggest that dialogue should account for a fixed proportion of the story – from a third up to two thirds, depending on the genre. Rules like that are often counterproductive, because the result becomes contrived and there are few things more tedious than unnecessary dialogue. Nevertheless, it is obviously a good idea to include dialogue in your story. Let it move the story on whenever possible. Use it to add pace and variety and give your characters more life and depth.

STAGE DIRECTIONS – WHO SAID WHAT AND HOW?

Many aspiring writers become worried about the repetition of 'he said/she said'. As a matter of fact, many of these worries are exaggerated. 'Said' has been described as 'almost invisible' and most of us can read a page of dialogue without seriously registering these words at all. Nevertheless, if you wish to avoid ending every paragraph with 'he said', there are some techniques that will assist.

1. Put the speech directions into a different place in consecutive paragraphs.

2. If there is a long speech, break it up and put your speech directions in the middle. Even quite short utterances often have a natural breathing space, and that makes an elegant place to note your speaker. So you could write:

> 'Hello, I'm Melanie', she said.
> She said, 'Hello, I'm Melanie.'
> or 'Hello,' she said, 'I'm Melanie.'

Do, in any case, watch your own prose and try to avoid using the same pattern all the time.

3. Another, often overlooked technique is simply to miss out the speaker altogether. The point has already been made that it should be evident who is speaking from the words he or she uses. One hardly needs to know the speech direction in the example above, for example, unless the speaker was not Melanie.

Even in connected dialogue, it is usually not necessary to name the speaker for several exchanges, and, the better your dialogue is, the less necessary it becomes. In any case, punctuation is on your side. Convention says that a new paragraph denotes a new speaker and, if you make the speeches short, this is usually enough to guide the reader, although if there are more than two speakers in the exchange it is more difficult.

You can ring other changes too. Call people by their names sometimes, or, if the viewpoint allows it, use a descriptive phrase ('the older man said') which will help to vary pace as well. Another elegant solution is to write other stage directions, showing what the character is doing, and omit the 'said'. The reader assumes that the character performing the action is also the speaker of the dialogue: '"I'm leaving", Peter stubbed out his cigarette.'

There are some tricks to avoid. Do not seek deliberate literary alternatives for 'said'. Your characters speak, they do not growl, hiss, splutter, shriek and drawl. They may quite reasonably 'reply', or even 'remark', but save emotional words such as 'whispered', 'cried' and 'snarled' for dramatic moments, and even then use them sparingly. A sentence such as '"I'm going to kill you", he hissed' is almost meaningless – try hissing it and see. Emotive words like this draw the reader's attention away from the dialogue and on to the speech directions, which is the opposite of what you want.

The same thing is true of adverbs which describe how words are said, especially those that end in '-ly'. Many authors try to heighten the effect by writing lines like this: '"I'm going to kill you", he said menacingly.' It does not take much imagination to see that the 'menacingly' here has almost no function at all. The words themselves are menacing, so the adverb is not adding anything. If you have a tendency to write supportive adverbs into your dialogue in this way, try taking them out and making the dialogue do the work.

Adverbs do have a useful role, however. They can be effective tools when they add something significant to the sense. Suppose our line of dialogue had said '"I'm going to kill you", he said lazily' (or 'cheerfully' or

61

'lovingly'). Here the adverb suggests a way of speaking which the reader does not automatically expect, and the effect can be quite striking, even sinister. Save your adverbs for this kind of use, and they will work for you.

CHECKPOINT 2

Try applying the following checklist to your dialogue:

1. Are people telling each other things that they already know?

2. Are they using appropriate register for the situation, and for the setting they are in?

3. Does each character have an individual 'voice' or do they all speak like each other or, worse still, like you? Does that voice 'fit' the character: that is, can I work out who is speaking without reading the speech directions?

4. Does every line of dialogue tell us something about one of the following:

• the character speaking
• another character
• the situation
• the background
• the mood
• the next step in the story
• another element in the plot?

If it does none of these things, it probably ought not to be there.

5. Does it successfully pretend to be conversation or does it sound contrived?

Study Box

We need no indication, in this extract, of who the speaker is. The content and speech patterns allow us to keep track of the dialogue throughout. (Note the use of action at the end, as a way of identifying the speaker.)

'Why would I sue her for divorce?'
'Because she's gonna sue you. We'll file first and allege that she deserted you in your hour of need.'
'Is that grounds for divorce?'
'No. But we'll also claim that you're crazy, temporary insanity. Just let me handle it. The McNaughten rule. I'm the sleazy divorce lawyer remember.'
'How could I forget?'
Jake poured hot beer from his neglected bottle and opened another.
John Grisham, *A Time to Kill*

Dickens understood how dialogue could appear to say one thing, and actually mean another. Here Mrs Sparsit makes her disapproval of Miss Gradgrind clear, not by anything she says, but by her facial expression, her pausing and her emphasis. Notice that Dickens does not tell us directly that she disapproves, he permits the clues in the dialogue to do the work.

'I think he married Gradgrind's daughter?'
'Yes,' said Mrs Sparsit, suddenly compressing her mouth. 'He had that – honour.'
'The lady is quite a philosopher, I am told?'
'Indeed, sir,' said Mrs Sparsit, '*Is she?*'
Charles Dickens, *Hard Times*

6. Can the dialogue actually be read aloud? Many writers fall into the trap of writing sentences of dialogue which would never be spoken because they are clumsy, complicated or ambiguous, or just plain difficult to say. There is only one way to find out. Read your dialogue aloud, like a play, and see whether it 'works'. Try to hear the 'voices' of your characters as you read.

Worksheet Four – Dialogue

You should by now have a clear picture of at least one central character. Before proceeding to this worksheet, it is preferable to repeat the earlier techniques for other locations and for other first-level viewpoint characters, if you have any. The greater the preparation for this activity, the more useful it is likely to be to the finished work.

1. Since 'hearing' dialogue depends upon an imagined 'audial' activity, it is helpful to begin by revisiting the meeting outlined in Worksheet Three. This time, however, as your viewpoint character goes to the meeting-point (whether accidental or otherwise), concentrate on sound. What sounds does your viewpoint character hear en route, or – if he doesn't move – just before the encounter takes place? Bring all your imaginative strategies into play, and ask yourself what effect the floor-covering (or lack of it) would have, and what activities you have mentally located in adjoining areas. Are there associated sounds?

2. When you are mentally alert for sound, allow the encounter to take place as before. (The same attitudes and mental description will prevail, but this time it is instantaneous.) Who speaks to whom, and exactly what is said? Try to capture in your mind the tone and calibre of voice and the manner of speech, as well as the actual words produced. Don't forget the body language, too – people who gaze into each other's eyes are intimate, those who avoid each other's gaze are sending other messages. Write the conversation down, remembering that it may not yet be dialogue.

3. Look over what you have written and decide if the register is right, both for the time and for the characters involved. Could you decide, without a doubt, which character is speaking when, even without the 'stage directions'? If not, look at it again. Unless your characters are very close in age, race, job, education and sex, their speech patterns should be widely different. (If you are unused to doing this, you may need to repeat the exercise several times before you begin to 'hear' the individual voices with clarity. Try getting someone else to read the extract, and see if they know – without your telling them – which speaker is which.)

4. Once you have mastered this, try a piece of proper dialogue; that is, an apparent conversation in which, as well as communicating to each other, the speakers communicate something to the reader. (If you find that you have done this already, so much the better!) At this point the snatch of dialogue can be something which you will introduce into your novel later on. If you find it difficult to differentiate between the speakers, when the words have to do two jobs at once, try reading your dialogue aloud, without the 'stage directions', preferably to someone else but just to yourself if necessary. Listen to yourself, and note the way in which you attempt to differentiate the voices – altering the pitch, the speed, the accent, and so on – and find ways to incorporate them into your prose. If you speak fast, make your speaker gabble, if slowly and ponderously – say that. Try to make the reader hear what you can mentally 'hear'.

5. As a check-back, write the information in the dialogue, as if you were passing it on to a friend yourself. Now look back: unless your major character is almost identical to you, the language and sentence structure should be different. If it isn't, read this section of the book again and keep experimenting.

6   PLOTTING

There will be sufficient plot, and it will not be wholly predictable. The structure of the story will be sufficiently clear for me to follow what is happening – even if (as in a thriller or a mystery) I do not know exactly what is causing it nor how different parts of the story interrelate. I shall, however, discover all this before the end. The plot will not require me to believe in strange coincidences, even if these have happened to the author in real life.

Reader contract

There is no one method for constructing plot. If you are writing a novel you probably already have ideas in mind, but here are some tried and tested strategies for working out a 'sufficient plot' and turning this into a narrative.

GETTING THE ORIGINAL IDEA

It is possible these days to purchase 'plot ideas', but this is neither necessary nor desirable. Your plot should arise directly from your characters and chart the effect which outward events have on their lives and their emotions and internal development. Well-constructed plots have five chief elements: People, Life-events, Obstacles, Theme, Shape, p-l-o-t-s. We have already examined how to create the characters from which the plot will spring. Let us now look at the life-events which form the storyline.

LIFE-EVENTS

These should be significant. Day-to-day routine does not make a plot, even if 'real life' is what the plot pretends to be. A novel demands dramatic moments of some kind, otherwise the narrative is dull to read. Of course, it is possible to have periods of contentment or boredom in your story, but it is difficult to keep the reader engaged with that for very long. That is why such scenes are usually sketched over in a paragraph or two, and romantic fiction, for example, tends to finish with the promise of marriage or of partnership rather than the actuality.

So what kind of 'life-event' might be significant? Georges Polti, a Frenchman writing in the eighteenth century, was a famous critic and commentator on the arts. He claimed that there were only a limited number (thirty-six) of dramatic situations in the world and that all plots were to a greater or lesser extent a reworking of one of those. Later commentators (even Goethe) have tried and failed to find satisfactory additions to his list, and you will notice that some of them are similar to each other in any case. Here – for reference – are the famous thirty-six dramatic situations which Polti asserted were the only possibilities. Note that there are several translations of this original French list, but this is the form in which I first encountered it.

1. Something longed for and denied
2. Delivery from some threat or circumstance
3. Crime pursued by vengeance
4. Revenge by one family member on another for real or imagined wrongs
5. Pursuit and the avoidance of pursuit
6. Disaster falling on a group or individual
7. Falling prey to cruelty or misfortune
8. Revolt against injustice or restraint
9. Daring enterprise
10. Abduction or kidnap
11. Facing a riddle or an enigma
12. Obtaining something or someone desired or undesired
13. Enmity between kinsmen
14. Rivalry between kinsmen for a single aim
15. Murderous, forbidden passion
16. Mental instability, including madness
17. Fatal imprudence
18. Involuntary crimes of love or passion
19. Premeditated crime for love or passion
20. Killing an unrecognized member of the family
21. Facing self-sacrifice for passion's sake
22. Facing self-sacrifice for an ideal (including patriotism)
23. Facing self-sacrifice for family
24. Necessary conflict of interest with one beloved
25. Rivalry within a hierarchy
26. Sexual infidelity, including adultery
27. Discovery of a loved one's dishonour
28. Love obstructed
29. Love for an enemy
30. Ambition
31. Conflict with destiny or with a god
32. Experiencing mistaken jealousy
33. Mistakenly judging of a person or event
34. Remorse
35. Recovery of a lost one
36. Loss of one beloved.

Five-Minute Exercise

Choose three novels which you have read. Which of the items on the list form the basis for the plots? Do they involve more than one of the above? Now think about the novel you intend to write, and ask yourself the same questions. Note that if one of these is not the driving force, you almost certainly need to rethink your plot.

Ensure that your plot has a dramatic situation of some kind, not necessarily a monumental matter of life and death, but with sufficient emotional tension and human interest to repay the investment of the reader's time. Avoid bizarre chance and strange coincidence, although these things do happen in real life. When an author creates them, the effect is inevitably contrived. 'Truth is stranger than fiction', at least in this respect. Fiction can only deal in what is credible. If your plot absolutely demands some such coincidence, at least try to make it as plausible as possible by showing the reader how it came about at every stage along the way. For instance, if it is essential that your hero accidentally meets – of all the men in London – the one individual whom he came to see (usually in some place where neither of them was supposed to be), then enable to the reader to follow the reasons, in advance, that will take both of them there together at that crucial time. If they just run across each other in a crowd, by chance, the reader is unlikely to believe it, and you will have breached the 'contract', even if there are dozens of real precedents in history.

In themselves the items on Polti's list are not 'sufficient plot'. Polti himself did not claim that they were plots at all, he called them dramatic situations from which all plots essentially derived. A plot shows how this dramatic situation works out through a series of events. Indeed, another interpretation of the *l* in *p-l-o-t-s* is *l*inks; think of the events in your story as the links in a chain, each leading to the next and each contributing to the strength of the whole.

If you experience a point in your writing where your plot seems to be stuck and nothing particular occurs to you, one way of arriving at an individual link is to ask yourself 'what if...?' questions about the situation, settings and characters so far. What if... this character ran away? What if... the apartment burned down? You can even practise by asking parallel 'what if...?' questions about events, people and places in your own life. If you can imagine the experience and how it would feel, it will give an emotional immediacy to your narrative. We shall return to the idea of links.

OBSTACLES

A plot is not a plot without some obstacle. Often this is implicit in the dramatic situation that you choose, but the precise form that the problem will take for your characters is up to you and, again, should be a product of the situation, setting and circumstances that you visualize. There may be a series of obstacles for your characters to face, but ensure that external events are not the only things to drive the plot. The development of the central characters is a crucial point. When the obstacles affect the lives of your fictitious people, it is how they cope with it which really makes the plot.

If they face a problem, they must solve it by their own efforts, not have things 'turn out right' by accident. If good fortune does smile on them, as it may do in the end, they must generally be shown to have deserved it in some constructive way, preferably by some use of their mental or physical capabilities, rather than by virtue of money, influence or rank. How they achieve this is really the substance of the plot. The more central the character, the more this is true. If the resolution is a tragic one, two possibilities arise. The character may be a 'pawn of fate', often the victim of someone else's misdeeds, or he may have brought the outcome on himself. There must still be 'effort', though, in either case: the pawn of fate may not deserve misfortune, but if the reader is to empathize with him there must be some attempt, if not to escape his fate, at least to achieve some other, worthwhile end. The character who wreaks his own destruction must do so actively. Tragedy which happens by default is hard to write successfully.

THEMES

Theme – the identification of some fundamental truth, image or idea which underpins the novel as a whole – is a fundamental element of plot. Some writing courses actually recommend beginning with the theme and then building plot and characters around that. However, this can easily distort the narrative. I do not believe in imposing a theme on a story, but in discovering the theme that is already there.

One way of identifying your underlying theme is to see whether there is an axiom, proverb or saying which your story could be said to illustrate. There are so many to choose from – 'pride goes before a fall', 'truth will out', and so on – that it is likely that one will occur to you. Sometimes, if your story has a sub-plot (*see below*) this may explore the very opposite idea from the one in the basic plot; and, since folk-wisdom is often contradictory, there is usually another axiom for that, 'look before you leap' in the main narrative may be contrasted, in a sub-plot, with 'strike while the iron is hot'. On the other hand, both these proverbs could be seen to relate to one idea, decision-making, and this leads us to another method of expressing theme. Take a single noun – justice, inheritance, rebellion, whatever is appropriate to your narrative – and keep this idea in mind when planning for your links. Having a theme like this can also help you to decide what kind of what-if questions you should ask yourself.

Another technique is to choose a single image from the natural world, ripples, for example. Obviously you would interpret this symbolically – a single action having wide effects – but it may also inform descriptive passages – a river, or the sea, or suggest a scene where someone drops a stone into a pond. Remember to treat this kind of image with restraint, so that it does not seem contrived, the effect is greatest when it is subliminal and the reader is not consciously aware of it.

Shape

A plot is also unlike 'real-life' in that it has a proper beginning, a middle and an end, and is not merely a series of events which happens to start and stop at certain points. It should have a dramatic development in the sense that it begins before or at a point of tension – one of Polti's dramatic situations or one of your what-if questions, probably – works through a period of change, tracing some development in the central characters as they face obstacles, and comes to some sort of resolution at the end. However, to maintain the tension and integrity of your chain of links until the end, more detailed techniques are desirable.

Identifying Plot-Points to Form Your Links

So you have decided what your dramatic situation is, what obstacles to solving this exist, what strategies your lead characters employ to counter these, and what final resolution you intend: you thus have the core elements of plot. However, even this is merely the skeleton on which the story hangs. Let us now turn to the actual events that will form the underpinning of the book and identify which scenes will form the links in your narrative chain.

The simplest way of doing this is to begin by breaking down your original ideas into no more than fifteen or twenty major elements of plot. These we shall call 'plot points' and once they are established they can be arranged and worked into the scenes that form your links, one or more to each chapter-plan, which will give you an overview of the narrative. It should also give you an idea of pace and indicate where more planning is required. You may even need to adjust the order of your plot-points as you go.

Let us take a concrete illustration and see how such plot-pointing might work in practice. Here is a beginner's first attempt at a synopsis for a romantic novel. It is chosen to illustrate a point, but the same principles apply in every genre, so please bear with the example given here. (Incidentally, the beginner in question is a published writer now, and has given permission for this to be used, provided that it remains anonymous.)

Faith has moved to London after an unhappy love affair. She joins a new company and meets the young, handsome boss, whom she finds very attractive. In the course of a number of business encounters she realizes that she is falling in love with him, and he dates her once or twice. Nevertheless, his fiery temper and his apparent attraction for Amanda, his red-haired secretary, make her insecure. However, when he rescues Faith's dog, risking his own life in the process, she realizes that he is the man for her. Amanda turns out to be merely an old flame and the two people come together in the end.

It is clear from this outline that the author sees the central relationship as an emotional journey rather than as something that develops through a series of actual happenings. In other words, there are not many life-events. There is really no concrete incident suggested anywhere until the final episode with the dog, and even that is extraordinarily vague. (What, exactly, happened to the dog?) We have discussed earlier the value of tying characters to a recognizable place and time, and it will instantly apparent that the vague 'joins a new company' scarcely qualifies for this, and the hero does not even have a name. We have the outline of an obstacle in Amanda, although no 'effort' by the lead character is involved in resolving this. What we have here may be the germinal idea for a story, but it is not yet a plot.

Turning the Outline into Links

The first step is to identify the plot-points as above: fifteen to twenty sentences, each of which contains one significant fact or incident. From the given outline we might render these points as:

• Faith has a broken love affair
• she comes to London
• she applies for a new job
• she goes to work
• she meets the boss
• she finds him attractive
• in the course of some business encounters she falls in love with him
• he dates her
• he proves to be fiery-tempered
• he seems to be very friendly with Amanda
• Faith is insecure in the relationship
• her dog gets into danger
• he rescues it, risking his life
• she realizes that he is for her
• Amanda turns out to be just an old flame
• Faith and her boss come together

It may seem rather tedious to spell it out like this, but it serves an important function in the planning process. A quick look down the list should make it clear where this plot is less than adequate. If we regard these points as potential links within a chain we can see that the first six relate to the beginning of the story or are simply background information anyway, while the last five relate to the resolution of the problem at the end. That leaves only five points for the whole middle of the story, which would, in fact, be seven-eighths of the book and most of them are general statements, rather than references to actual events. Our chain is far too weak in the centre. Listing your plot-points shows up vague planning of this kind.

Turning Plot-Points into Scenes

Plot-points in this form are not yet links. To arrive at this, we must turn them into scenes, each of which will form an individual link within the chain. There may be more than one link per chapter and we need to spread the load throughout the narrative. This will necessitate combining some of the initial points, expanding others and treating some as background information. Where the outline is particularly vague we may have to ask additional questions to strengthen it or plan additional links so that the chain is strong throughout. Our chain of linking scenes might begin like this, for instance:

• Faith goes for an interview (as what?, where?)
• she goes to work at her new job; she meets the new boss (where?, how?, what is his name?) and thinks him attractive (in what way?)
• she discovers his friendship with Amanda (how?)

and so on; doubtless you will see at once how much more like a possible story even this simple plot starts to become when treated in this way. It also shows which plot-points will not make proper links at all. The several business encounters mentioned in the outline are in this category The idea is so vague that it cannot be crammed into a single scene, and there is insufficient information to make a chapter out of each. Much more detailed planning is required here. Envisaging your plot-points as individual scenes in this way is a good way of giving the story some real shape, and showing where more planning is required.

You will also note that the first two of the original plot-points do not occur at all. The advice of the King in *Alice in Wonderland* that one should 'begin at the beginning, go on to the end and then stop' does not apply. Background information, what might be called 'the story before the story', is often more usefully revealed in the course of the action than painstakingly spelled out in the first paragraphs. In fact, looking at that list of scenes again, we are able to adjust the starting point. Unless something happened at that interview which is important to the plot, it clearly makes sense to begin this story later still, at the moment where she arrives at her new job. If she does that, we know that she was interviewed and got the post, otherwise she would not be here, and, by eliminating that first scene altogether, we have made the meeting of the hero and heroine – a dramatic high point in any romantic novel – happen sooner in the narrative. Think of this as 'taking up the slack' and making the chain of scenes more strong and taut.

Moving on, the lack of links within the central part shows us that many more scenes are required. We can use the original criteria to decide what these might be. In the outline Faith shows no development as a character. What effort does she make to overcome the obstacles? What if she learns to stand up to her boss? Could we have a scene or two in which this gradually occurs? Also, if we can identify the theme, that will guide us in strengthening the plot. Suppose we take 'things are not always what they seem' as being a statement of the theme (it is an honourable one: the theme of *Pride and Prejudice* could be expressed in the same words), can we apply this to create new scenes? Start by asking 'what if...?' questions again. What if Amanda is not what she seems, in other senses than the romantic one? What if the job itself is not what it seems? Should all this fail, we can always turn back to Polti's list and introduce another dramatic situation into the chain.

The time taken to do this kind of planning is worthwhile, at least until you are familiar with the craft. Innumerable novels are begun and then abandoned halfway through because the storyline gets 'stuck' – the author cannot see how to maintain the plot, and all those hours of writing-time are wasted. This can be avoided if you have at least a general overview of where the major plot-points are, how to turn them into scenes and ensure that there are sufficient links to support your narrative chain until the end. The process will also give

---

Five-Minute Exercise

1. Think of the Cinderella story again. Try to pick out the plot-points for the narrative (no more than twenty at most) including the story before the story. Where does the narrative traditionally begin?
2. What are the major plot-points in your novel? Where have you begun the narrative? Can you turn your plot-points into scenes? Are there enough links in the middle section to maintain the narrative?

you the basis for a synopsis, later on, when you come to submit your manuscript to a publisher.

Other Uses for Your Plot-Point Links and Scenes

Plotting the story in this way has other advantages as well. For one thing it enables you to arrange material so as to set the scene for later elements. For instance, in the example plot above, in order to bring about the crucial plot-point with the dog, it is important that Faith has a dog, that she is fond of it, and that it occasionally gets into scrapes. There should probably therefore be an early scene where the dog gets into momentary danger and Faith gets upset. This may not be important for the love affair, but it is important for the *plot*, because otherwise the dog will appear to the reader to be one of those coincidental devices that we talked about, introduced merely to be rescued by the boss.

Writing-in such material to prepare the way is known as 'seeding', because one sows the seeds of future elements of the plot. It is an important technique indeed. Identifying your plot-points in advance will enable you to decide not only what information you need to seed in advance, but where to do this in order to produce the maximum effect.

In our imaginary novel we could have Faith learn about Amanda's friendship with the boss by listening to the gossip of the other girls. This would serve several purposes: it would help to create the office atmosphere; it would introduce Amanda as a femme fatale before she appears upon the scene herself (the reader will always believe the characters rather than what the author says), and by using the unreliable witness technique we can set up the idea of the romantic liaison which does not really exist, without making Faith look like an idiot. If Amanda is merely another character whom Faith meets in the normal course of things,

much of this impact would be lost. Use your plot-points to work out appropriate moments to seed your own important information in this way.

CHECKPOINT 1

Look at your own plot-outline from this point of view. Is there any information for a later scene which you need to seed in advance?

How Plot-Pointing Can Help You to Obscure an Element of Plot

If you are writing a thriller or mystery you may want to achieve the opposite effect. Then you can use your plot-points to help you to disguise a fact. It is part of the reader contract that all significant information should be divulged before the end, but a seeded fact may easily be missed if it is introduced casually in a scene before we know that it might be significant. For example, if the taxi left at 10 o'clock, write a scene where someone mentions that – among other things – before we discover that the taxi and the time are vital clues. The greater the distance between the two events, the greater the disguise.

That phrase 'among other things' is significant here, because any item hidden in a list will often be ignored: Agatha Christie, for example, relies on this in several instances. This explains why an extended physical description of a scene is often part of detective writing and why characters in such books sometimes seem to chatter in inconsequential ways, in apparent contravention of what has been said elsewhere. The detail and the chit-chat may camouflage a clue. In the same way, it has been said that you can give the reader almost any important fact by having someone say it just before a man bursts in with a gun – the reader will then focus on the action, rather than on the moments that preceded it.

71

Looking at your plot-points in advance will help you to decide where techniques like this can most effectively be used.

KEEPING VARIATION IN THE PLOT

Once you are convinced that you have sufficient links it is also important to ensure that the storyline is not so similar in tone throughout that it becomes monotonous. For instance, in the plot-outline we have been looking at, those business encounters could be quite a large proportion of the plot. The idea of a series of chapters based on this, however, is not acceptable. Of course, one or two of the most significant encounters might be planned in detail, taking care that they are quite different from each other and that each moves the emotional plot on a little in some way. There might be some emotional contrast between these episodes, one being apparently successful, another leaving our heroine feeling low. (The failure of the original 'synopsis' to suggest this kind of change of mood is a serious fault.) A plot-line needs some emotional ups and downs to keep the reader interested, and that applies to lightweight romance as much as to gripping adventure stories and gritty contemporary drama.

Even given emotional light and shade, however, these business scenes would not make good successive chapter-scenes, because they would provide too much similarity in the narrative in terms of situation, setting and character. This is where plot-points can help again. If successive chapters seem too similar, it is time to take active steps to introduce some variety.

CHECKING FOR EMOTIONAL VARIETY

There are many techniques for gauging the emotional content of a plot, and your preferred method will probably depend upon your imaginative style. Perhaps the best way of determining which works for you is to try out each of them in turn and see which you find the most illuminating.

Take the Cinderella story as an example once again, because it is a short story and therefore manageable. If we break it down into plot-point scenes, as usual, we can then award each scene an emotional mark out of ten, where ten is a moment of high pleasure and one is near-despair. So, at the outset, we might award a mark of three or four, rising a little when the letter comes, dropping to the bottom when the sisters leave, rising sharply when the fairy godmother appears. The plot-points may then be charted in a star system of this kind. You may arrive at slightly different conclusions, but that is immaterial. Only the general principle matters here.

1. Cinderella tends the sisters   ****
2. The letter comes   ******
3. Cinderella cannot go   **
4. She has to help the sisters   ***
5. They set off, leaving her alone   *
6. The fairy godmother arrives   ********
7. She arranges the dress, etc.   **********
8. She warns Cinderella about
      12 o'clock   ***
9. Cinderella goes to the ball   *********
10. She meets the prince and they
      fall in love   ***********
11. The clock strikes twelve   *

And so on. The emotional variety is evident. Note that before that highest point there is a momentary low, making the high points higher by contrast, and this is an important narrative device. Too many high spots or chapters of unrelieved despair are generally not successful. Tragedy cuts deeper when it follows hope, and happiness is greatest when it transcends despair, as storytellers have known

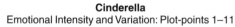

Cinderella
Emotional Intensity and Variation: Plot-points 1–11

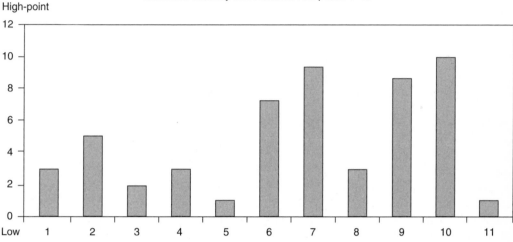

Cinderella – plot-pointed (musically) 1–11

for generations. Read any good book of your chosen genre, and you will almost certainly find this principle in operation there. Many authors use a system such as this, sometimes converting it into a graph (*see top diagram*).

At least one audial thinker that I know treats each star-rating as a musical note and turns the plot-line into a kind of tune. Here, one star might equate with middle C, two stars with D and so on up to top E. This seems to be particularly effective if the volume varies together with the note (*see bottom diagram*).

Five-Minute Exercise

As a brief exercise, try 'starring' the rest of the Cinderella story for yourself. Plot it as a graph, and hum it as a tune. Which of these techniques works better for you?

Apply the same exercise to your plot, or to any other story that you have written. Are there any points where more variety is obviously required?

Using Sub-Plots

One way of creating such variety is to introduce a sub-plot into your narrative. In longer and more complex novels these will almost certainly occur naturally. A sub-plot is a secondary story which impinges on the central characters in some way: often it relates to other aspects of their lives, but sometimes other characters are the primary participants. Generally, this story runs through most of the novel, although there are examples of 'mini-plots', especially in episodic or adventure novels where the secondary story is introduced and resolved within a short period.

A sub-plot may be an undercurrent, for instance, in a novel with a social theme, where we follow the plight of one unhappy individual who is tangential to the central plot. This kind of sub-plot may be quite low-key and have few scenes actually devoted to it. We discover what happens largely through allusion and dialogue and may have to deduce the outcome for ourselves. At other times sub-plots are more parallel to the main story: often the adventures of a friend, relative or associate of one of the first-level characters. This story may be linked thematically to the central plot or have emotional or practical effects for the protagonists, and, if so, may be a much larger feature of the book. As has already been mentioned, the main actors in a sub-plot of this kind may make good viewpoint characters, especially for those sections of the book devoted to this part of the story.

We have seen that sub-plots may echo the main storyline or theme or be deliberately contrastive in order to give pace and variety to the whole. The love-interest in a thriller or a spy story usually comes into this category, while romances often profit from some sub-plot of action or intrigue. (In the simple plot-outline we looked at earlier, a lively sub-plot on some other theme – business malpractice for example – would have added a great deal.)

There may be more than one sub-plot in a book. Consider again *Pride and Prejudice.* There are clearly several sub-plots there – Charlotte Lucas, Lydia, Jane – all of which impinge on Elizabeth, but only in a secondary way. Espionage and stories of intrigue almost invariably have two or three minor plots like this, while sagas and other longer genres may have many more. Sub-plot heroes and heroines, where they are not the main protagonists of the novel, do not have to develop in the same way as the central ones, nor is their effort necessarily required. In *Pride and Prejudice* Jane and Lydia do not alter greatly, and much of their happiness is achieved by the 'efforts' of the main protagonists, rather than by their own deserving acts.

Sub-plots, then, not only give a wider picture, they add tension and interest. If your first effort at plot-pointing scenes suggests that there is insufficient substance in your intended plot, consider the possibility of introducing some such secondary element.

There are occasional novels with genuine twin-plots, two stories, of equal significance, which become entwined or prove to relate to one another in the end. In this case, guidelines for sub-plots do not apply: one story may be told, and then the other, without the need to integrate the two, the denouement does exactly that. However, this is an unusual event and very often a literary effect. For most authors, it is necessary to decide what is the main plot, and what is, or are, subsidiary to that.

Methods for Arriving at a Sub-Plot

A sub-plot may occur to you at once, but, if not, the usual strategies apply. One obvious starting-point is Polti's list. If your central plot seems rather thin, weaving in another dramatic situation – whether relating to your lead characters or not – will help. Remember that the sub-plot will also need to be resolved, although not necessarily as fully as your central storyline.

If no immediate idea occurs to you from this, ask yourself some 'what if...?' questions about your minor characters: 'What if this character is taken ill? Proves untrustworthy? Has a hidden past?' Or you may try a visualization exercise like the one outlined below. For most writers one of these strategies will throw up new ideas. If this means that a low-level role assumes a new importance in the plot, you will naturally have to devote a little time to developing that character more fully.

Do not forget to use your theme to give your story unity. Supposing that you are writing a historical romance and have chosen pride, for instance, as your central theme. Your sub-plots may then examine other kinds of pride, either positive – humble pride, pride in others, pride in family honour or accomplishments – or pride in its more destructive forms, vanity, conceit or egotism. You can use this irrespective of whether your sub-plot springs direct from the central storyline or whether you have gone back to Polti's list and used your 'what-if' questions to manufacture one. In this way, all parts of the story will cohere. Sub-plots and minor characters fit into the grand scheme. In fact, and this is a bonus of using theme, it becomes much easier to delineate your minor characters, because you can ask yourself 'How does the person illustrate the theme?' In our imaginary historical romance, even the little kitchen maid may be shyly proud of her young man while the neighbouring landlord could be proud of his hideous, haughty and unaccomplished daughter.

CONCRETE VISUALIZATION

Close your eyes and visualize a scene that you have planned. Let the scene run through your mind in the usual way: imagine the place, the

---

Five-Minute Exercise: Using 'What-if?' Ideas

1. Make a list of six minor characters in your intended plot. (If you have not got this far with your planned novel, use the characters in some well-known fairy story instead. The effect is obviously not the same, but it will help you become familiar with the exercise.)

2. Now jot down three 'what-if?' questions randomly. Write down the first ones that occur to you. Try to find questions of your own if possible – Polti's list may help you in this task. Now apply these questions to each character in turn.

3. Now go back to your plot-point scenes and ask yourself some 'what-if' questions about four of them.

Which lines seem to you the most promising?

---

people, listen to what is said and try to capture any sounds and scents. Now realize that there was someone else who witnessed this as well, someone you had not noticed until now. Who is it? Where is he? What is he doing there? What will he do now, and what difference will that make to the plot?

A PLOT-LINE, NOT A STRAITJACKET

There is one more important point. Because you have identified your chain of scenes, established your theme and worked out your subsidiary plot, you are not compelled to follow this plan slavishly. As you write, you may wish to adapt, embellish or even change your original ideas, even in some cases when you have already written them. Do not be afraid of this. Certainly it is tiresome, when one has struggled to the end of a carefully written chapter, to look at the next plot-points and suddenly see a different way of achieving the maximum effect, but it is an indication that your plot has life. Published authors do this all the time, and successful published authors most of all. (This is where a word-processor is such a boon.)

Occasionally you may find that a character, faced with the next action you had planned for him, simply refuses to comply. This is usually a product of sketchy characterization at the start, an indication that you did not know the person well enough. However, reaching this point is an indication that you understand him now. If you feel strongly that this character would not do that, then listen to your inner prompting and find some other way of bringing things to pass. It may mean fresh plot-pointing at this stage, but it will be time profitably spent. Otherwise the plot-line will seem forced. Sometimes the opposite thing occurs. You may find that a detail you introduced, for no very good reason, in Chapter 3 suddenly acquires significance and can become a pivot of the plot. If this happens, welcome it as a present from the muse. Most writers have encountered this phenomenon at some time. Certainly you should not ignore it because it was not 'in the plan'.

It is probable that when you picked up this book you already some sort of story-line in mind. Remember, however, that a simple story-line is not yet a plot, we need to find the p-l-o-t-s: People, Life-events, Obstacles, Themes and Shape.

1. People: If you have worked through the other worksheets, you should now be in a position mentally to see and hear your characters and place them in a series of specific and fully rounded settings. That is the first element of plot.

2. Life-events. Look at Polti's list again, and see which of his 'life-events' are the basis for your intended plot. There should be at least three of these, so if you have only one or two it would be a good idea to find another, and find a way of either introducing it into your main story-line or creating a sub-plot in which it occurs. However, it is rarely satisfactory to 'select' a life-event and then simply try to graft it onto your existing plot. Start with the people once again (not necessarily the major characters) and ask which of the remaining list seem most likely to affect them. Then, simply as an exercise, go back and work out how at least two other life-events could be introduced, without being either wholly predictable or beyond belief. (It is not, of course, necessary to include these in your finished work.)

3. Revert to the major characters that you have created in the greatest detail. What emotional, financial, professional, personal or social effects will your plot elements have on them? Try to 'think yourself' into their frame of mind when these life-events occur – place them, if possible, in the scene which you have worked on, and let them look at it again. What, as they look around that self-same space, do they now see and think? Do the same thing for the other, minor character. What effect, if any, does this have on him or her? Jot down your thoughts – you may find them the basis for writing the scene later on.

4. Obstacles: You have probably decided on the major obstacles. However, do remember that not all are physical. Try to think of an emotional or social barrier as well; or, if these are the basis of your plot, try introducing a physical impediment. A small thing – a locked door, bad weather, barking dogs – can carry considerable emotional effect. List the obstacles that you envisage and indicate the kind of 'effort' required from your lead characters to bring about the resolution you intend. The effort may also be of different types, usually matching the kind of obstacle, but should also produce development in your major characters – what kind of development do you propose, and how will this manifest itself?

5. Theme: What do you consider to be your major theme? Is there an axiom that sums it up? Or a natural image? Whichever you consider it to be, first write it down, and then decide on a particular scene that explicitly exemplifies the theme. Outline at least one scene for each first-level character and – if possible – one from a sub-plot which exemplifies it for a second or third-level one.

6. Shape. As this is your first novel, it is important that you have some idea, at this stage, how each obstacle will be resolved, and what the final outcome will be for each of the major characters. Endings can be of different kinds: positive (in which all obstacles are neatly solved); grim (in which the obstacles triumph); or occluded, in which the reader is deliberately left in doubt. This last is usually an apparently 'positive' ending carrying the seeds of its own destruction; or a hope, however slight, modifying a grim or tragic end. What is not available – for a beginning novelist at any rate – is an inconclusive end, in which the story simply peters to a stop.

7. Insofar as you able, use the notes above to create the major plot-points for your story. (At least twelve, but one for each chapter is a good idea.)

7 PLANNING CHAPTERS

The story will keep me interested until the end. It will not tail off in the middle nor wander off on the author's hobby horse, nor will the plot take half the volume to begin.

Reader contract

OPENINGS ARE VITAL

We saw in our consideration of the Faith story in the last chapter the importance of beginning the first chapter with action, and at an appropriate plot-point. This is more than a technical matter. The opening of your novel is of paramount importance. It is, after all, the moment at which any reader – including a publishing editor – decides whether or not to carry on with the book. How often have you picked up a novel, glanced at the first page or two and decided that this was or was not for you?

Most first-time writers are aware of this, and therefore they often write and rewrite the opening scene a dozen times before they move on to writing anything else. There are two strong reasons for not doing this. Almost certainly you will develop ideas and details as you write and you may discover information later on that could be usefully seeded in this opening. Indeed, even if your novel is accepted your editor may wish you to rewrite this part again. Also, because so much energy has been expended on this early scene, later chapters tend to be more sketchy and mechanical, or the author gives up altogether in despair of ever making progress with the book. So write the scene as well as you are able, and then move on. It will be all the better for revision later on when you will, after all, be more practised at your craft.

With this caveat in mind, where do you begin? We have already touched on the desirability of beginning the story with action of some kind, rather than by giving all the necessary background information for the plot. But how do you choose a plot-point as a starting place?

WHERE TO START: THE 'POINT OF CRISIS' PRINCIPLE

A useful precept is to choose a scene at, or immediately before, some major point of crisis or change. It has long been accepted in detective fiction that a manuscript with a body in the first chapter has more chance of success than one without, but the same principle applies to any genre. The 'crisis moment' ensures that there is a degree of tension straightaway, and – whether that is murder, a new flat or a political revolution – the reader is caught up in it at once. Beginning your story with a powerful event is a useful way of capturing the imagination and ensuring involvement with your tale.

The opening will set the general mood. As a rule of thumb, the more dramatic the crisis, the more serious the tone of the novel. Even a romantic novel which opens with a death (of the heroine's parent, for example) sets a mood of darkness and social realism. If you begin a thriller with a threat you promise a tense narrative: a story that begins with a journey suggests emotional upheaval, and so on.

Choosing the moment immediately *before* a point of change lacks that initial impact, but it has values of another kind. For one thing, it enables you briefly to evoke the 'way things were'. This can be emotionally quite powerful, since it gives the reader a glimpse of what is to be lost or under threat. (If your abductor threatens a mother's small children in the park, the impact is greater if we first see her playing happily with them and taking carefree joy for granted. It also establishes how much she cares and how vulnerable the children are, both of which are important factors in the plot.) If you do choose this method it is important, in general, to keep this first scene brief and as potently written as you can manage it, otherwise the crisis, when it comes, will lose much of its effect.

If there is no suitable and obvious early crisis in your storyline, you may wish to create an external one, so that your narrative commences with a bang. What you choose will naturally depend upon the type of novel you are writing. Hence, if yours is a historical novel based in Elizabethan times, you might invent a scene in which your hero or heroine runs into some dramatic aspect of Tudor life which is germane to your central theme or plot. It might be an execution, if threat of injustice threatens one of your characters at some time; a royal procession, if affairs of court or rags-to-riches is to be your theme; or

some hapless individual being whipped, if you are concerned with social conditions and personal injustice.

Do remember, however, that this opening incident must be woven into the story afterwards. Your hero cannot simply happen across an execution and then go home, it must affect his life, emotions or interests in some way, or pave the way for something else to come. Look for ways in which your character can meet someone or see something in that scene which seeds the way for further incident.

In general, short sentences, brief paragraphs, action and dialogue make for an eye-catching and gripping opening. If a more literary or dreamy opening is desired, this can be achieved by longer sentences and passages of description or internal dialogue. However, this requires considerable skill and is difficult to maintain for long. 'Dreamy' becomes 'dreary' very readily. Another consideration for an opening scene is the number of characters involved. The question of how many of your cast to introduce within the first few pages can be a real concern. Too many and you confuse the reader. Too few and you are in danger of lacking pace, unless your opening scene is a dramatic one.

If you have difficulty with this, there are some general rules of thumb. It is wise to introduce at least one of your lead characters. There may be secondary characters as well, but probably no more than two or three, depending on the kind of novel that you write. Note, however, that this applies to *characters*: it does not mean that you should have only three or four people in the scene. There may be crowds of them, as in that execution earlier, but only a few will be individualized, and only first- or second-level characters will be truly 'introduced'. Also, if there are two lead characters, in a romance, for instance, it is wise to give the reader at least a glimpse of the second one fairly early on.

All this is fairly standard counsel, but it is not unknown for a novelist to flout it quite successfully, or to follow it and then to have a publishing editor request the opposite – for instance, that more of the characters should be introduced at once. Nonetheless, it remains the best advice. In order to reach that editor at all, it is better not to overcrowd the stage. Introduce a few characters and have them act.

WEAVING IN THE 'BACK-PLOT': SOME STYLISTIC POINTS

But to plunge your characters into action from the start raises other problems. How does the reader discover what has come before, the essential 'back-plot' from which this action stems, and which will probably form the first few items of your plot-point list? Some classical writers, after all, introduce their characters and background first, and only then begin the action of the novel. Why cannot modern novels do the same? This is more than transient literary fashion, I believe. Film and television have again had a role to play, by altering the way a story is perceived. A film begins by plunging the audience straight into events, and modern readers, skilled in watching films, have become adept at interpreting unspoken clues and picking up a story in the middle by discovering background information bit by bit.

Patient introductory exposition is not needed now. Worse, research into reading habits suggests that, even in authors such as Dickens, it is often skipped by readers nowadays, and regarded as being tedious. This creates a challenge for the author, naturally. It is necessary to begin with some compelling scene, and yet ensure that vital background information will emerge. The 'readers' assumptions' may assist you here to some extent, but if you set your story in some other time and place, there may be a great deal your readers need to understand about different customs, climate, costume, laws and all the rest. In any case, they will need to know about the background of the individual characters, their relationship to one another and what events have happened previously to bring these people to this 'point of change'.

This is not quite the same as depicting 'character', but many of the techniques are just the same. Characters can give clues in dialogue, sometimes of a simple kind. A man who enquires, 'How's your wife?' indicates that he is talking to a married man. The answer, ' No better, I'm afraid. The doctors doubt that she'll survive the birth' would fill us in with back-plot straightaway. A viewpoint character can give clues by what he thinks:

> Keith was there. It made her uncomfortable. He was a good agent, Barney said, but she had never liked Keith Wallace since the day he had tried to seize her in the lift and press his fat sensuous lips against her throat.

Or by what he 'remembers':

> He tried to recall what he knew of her. Thirty-six. Unmarried. Said to be a prickly customer. Leading photographer within her field. Fearless too. Once saw off an Arab tribesman with a gun – or so the legend said ...

Linking narrative can give brief pieces of information direct: 'Leif Henriksson came in, fresh from his posting to the New York Branch.' (Note that where there is a third-person narrative character, this is often effectively 'what the character thinks', as well.)

One basic principle underlies all these techniques: where possible, feed the information in a little at a time. Big blocks of information tend to be exactly that, big blocks, both to the

Study Box

Here are two 'back-plot' examples, which may also show how the techniques that we have been examining come together in a scene. The first example is a simple one. Speaking to a confidante, a young woman reveals a significant back-plot event. Note the way the dialogue is constructed, with the important point being highlighted by a pause (created when the speaker sips her drink) so that the reader has time to take it in.

> '... I steeled myself to his attacks and stuck it out, hoping and praying he would never come back whenever he went to London. He always did. When I was almost twelve he finally went, well, he went the whole way, Anya. He raped me one Saturday afternoon when my mother was in Edinburgh with Sandy.'
>
> Kay stopped again, took a sip of tea. After a few moments she murmured, 'That happened several times.'
>
> Barbara Bradford Taylor,
> *Three Weeks in Paris*

In the next extract we see a real tour de force. Ian Rankin uses the device of a police briefing, both to give us some of the back-plot facts, and also to let us know that there is something troubling about them to Rebus, the viewpoint character in this 'apparent third-person' narrative. A piece of dialogue (in appropriate informative register) is spoken by a secondary character and gives information about past events. There is far too much information for one speech, however, so it is interrupted, first by Rebus's thoughts – some of which are given in italics, as direct stream-of-consciousness – and also by physical events. Note how the photograph is used to give a visual dimension. (Of course, to the casual reader, none of this technique is obvious.)

> 'Take a look. His name is Eric Lomax.' Rebus knew the name. His heart missed a beat. 'Beaten to death with something resembling a baseball bat or pool cue. Hit with such force that splinters of wood were embedded in the skull.' The photo landed in front of Rebus. it showed the body at the scene of crime, an alleyway illuminated by the photographer's flash, raindrops falling into puddles. Rebus touched the photo, but didn't pick it up, afraid that his hand might tremble. *Of all the unsolveds still mouldering in their boxes and storerooms why did it have to be this one?* He focused on Tennant, seeking a clue.
>
> 'Eric Lomax,' Tennant was saying, 'died in the centre of our biggest, ugliest city on a busy Friday night. Last seen a bit the worse for wear, leaving his usual pub. About five hundred yards from this alley ...'
>
> Ian Rankin, *Resurrection Men*

reader's participation and to the forwarding of the narrative. If necessary (where, for example, there is too much information to impart in 'internal monologue') write a paragraph containing all the background information that you require and then deliberately interrupt that with other dialogue or action by your characters. As we noted earlier, merely adding a phrase like 'He put down his glass' will do much to return the scene to the narrative 'present' instead of keeping the reader focused on the past.

Avoiding the Overuse of 'Had'

One simple technique you can apply is to count how many times the past perfect tense appears: that is, the two-part, past tense verb form that begins with 'had' – 'had done', 'had lived' or even the perfectly correct, but unhappy form 'had had' ('He had had ten years' training in the art...'). This tense with 'had' is used only for action that took place before the central time-frame of the narrative ('His wife had died ten years before'). This makes it the archetypal back-plot tense. If you find that you have used it more than two or three times in successive sentences, it is probably time to introduce some action with no 'had' – 'he put down his glass' – which brings us back to narrative reality. Technically, this latter tense is called the simple past, and is the fundamental story-telling tense in English prose.

Sometimes in longer paragraphs you may find it possible to drop the 'had' after the first few instances:

> She had been beautiful. He remembered the first time he saw her. She was walking up the steps of the Institute, her long hair flying, and laughing with the plump girl at her side. She was wearing red that day, in defiance of convention, a beacon of irreverence in that stuffy place. He had lost his heart to her at once.

You can perhaps see that we have a small flashback here. For a sentence or two we are transported into the thinker's imagination, where we can watch the memory played out before our eyes. It would, of course, be entirely possible to write that scene using the 'had' tense throughout ('... the first time he had seen her. She had been walking...'). However, the effect is subtly different. This makes us observers of a previous event, rather than sharers of a present memory. Note that it is usually necessary to return to the 'had' form for the final verb to signal a return to the narrative's 'real time'. If managed properly, this kind of flashback can be a success. Readers do not seem to notice that the narrative has been interrupted by the past. However, the technique cannot easily be sustained for long. It is best confined to a single memory, and to one paragraph at a time.

Incorporating Longer Flashback Scenes

There are occasions when the storyline demands that a more extended piece of back-plot must be given. One simple device for doing this is to have one of the characters relate the story to another. However, do make sure in doing this that the recital is not made to someone who already knows the facts (unless the narrator is deliberately deceived in this), that it is told in a way which fits the character, and, finally, that the story is not told at length without some interruption or relief, if only by a brief comment or question by the listener. Alternatively, it is possible to write such scenes in flashback narrative. This is a more complicated strategy, and may have drawbacks or advantages depending on how and when it is used.

Unless it is used for special purposes, flashback scenes inevitably delay the narrative. There are times when the author can exploit this fact, but not at the beginning of the manuscript. It is sometimes said that the first page or two of most beginners' novels could be torn up with advantage since most of it is back-plot anyway, and often in extended, flashback form. If your manuscript begins like this, with scenes which are mostly 'what happened up till now', think carefully about how this might be managed differently. The modern reader wants to get on with the plot, not spend time on what led up to it.

However, there are occasions when such flashback may be used to great effect, for instance, in psychological suspense or where there is some element of mystery, with a character withholding or suppressing memory. Here, flashback sequences may be introduced, often in italics or some other, distinctive style to indicate that this is memory of another time and place, and as a simple parallel narrative, thus avoiding the use of 'had'. Sometimes the present tense is used! There is no attempt to disguise or minimize these sequences, they simply interrupt the on-going narrative (although it may well emerge that something in that narrative triggered them). They may vary in length from a sentence or two to several pages and may at first seem incoherent to the reader. However, as the narrative progresses, the fragments increasingly coalesce, so that in the end a total picture is revealed. You will see that the withheld memory in this instance has become the 'enigma explained' from Polti's list, and thus is an essential part of plot.

Other genres, such as mystery or espionage, may also withhold a background scene or scenes like this and present them as flashback later on, because it is necessary for the plot that the whole truth is not revealed at once. However, note that in these cases the flashback is not usually at the beginning of the book, but is used intentionally to interrupt the on-going narrative.

BEGINNING CHAPTERS OTHER THAN THE FIRST

It is tempting to suppose that the techniques for writing the beginning of the book could apply equally to the beginning of any subsequent chapter. And so, of course, they could – except that we must remember the importance of contrast and variety. If every chapter begins with a dramatic incident, the reader will soon begin to notice this and feel that every opening is the same. This makes the narrative seem predictable, in contravention of the reader contract. Try instead to create a variety of chapter openings. You might, for instance, vary the narrative technique: begin one chapter with dialogue, the next with action and the one after that with a sentence or two of description of a scene.

You might use variety of mood, not only at the start of chapters, but in the relationship between them in the manuscript. If one chapter closes with a happy scene, begin the next one on a sombre note; if you conclude with tension, open the next chapter with respite. This gives the narrative variety and is particularly easy to achieve if you have more than one viewpoint character. Or you may achieve the contrast that you need simply by switching to a different scene or to another element of plot.

Think back to the point-of-tension charts we looked at earlier. You will recognize how high-points contrast best with low. If there is a great deal of tension in your story, unrelieved, it will be less effective than a plot-line that permits an intermediate, brief period of calm. A lot of low-level contentment will be hard to read unless it is contrasted with some flash of threat or moment of high emotional charge.

This is where a sub-plot comes into its own. A high point in one plot may contrast nicely with a tranquil moment in another. Or a simple change of viewpoint narrator may do the trick: an event which threatens tragedy and ruin to one person may be a source of innocent excitement to the next. Sometimes the opposite strategy applies. End a chapter in the middle of a scene, by selecting a moment when something significant is said or done and finish there. The next paragraph simply picks up the plot again, so tension is maintained across the chapter break. This may be extended further by combining these techniques. Reaching a climactic moment in the plot, the author does not resolve it instantly but ends the chapter there and switches to another scene or character. This device leaves the reader wanting to read on and can be very effective if not overdone – once or twice in a novel is probably enough. In general, contrasts in location, characters or mood across a chapter break create variety and speed the narrative; linking them results in a more deliberate pace.

CLOSING A CHAPTER

It will be seen from this that finishing a chapter is just as important as beginning it, and many of the same principles apply. Take care that every chapter closes differently. Readers are particularly alert to this – probably, once again, as a result of the cinema. We are all familiar with children's television series in particular, where every episode resolves itself almost identically. Oddly, many beginner writers fail to see this trap and have a tendency to finish every chapter in a similar way, with a murder or a wisecrack, a question or a kiss, or whatever is appropriate to the genre.

It is possible to close a chapter at the end of an incident, in which case you 'resolve' it there and you can pick up the next scene without a link. Or you can close when the incident is unresolved, in which case a good place to stop is the moment when a threat is introduced or a significant new character arrives. This heightens tension and keeps the reader eager to know what happens next.

Note all the high-spots in the narrative, and place one near the end of a chapter occasionally. Or use a 'low' moment to create a sombre mood. Whatever you decide, the chapter must have shape: it is not sufficient to stop a chapter simply because it is getting rather long. Plot the ends of chapters carefully and devote as much to them as to the opening. Some writers even find it useful now and then to start with the last paragraph of a scene and then write up to that, although this is not a technique that suits everyone.

USING THE SPACES BETWEEN CHAPTERS

Chapter-breaks may have a useful function in themselves. They can avoid dead-time in the narrative. There may be a transitional period of several days or even years when nothing very notable occurred. There may be a long journey, a tedious business meeting or hours of fruitless searching for a friend. If so, it is not necessary to chronicle all this. Simply end one chapter when the event begins and start the next when it is over, at the first subsequent, important incident.

If your story included such a journey, for example, the following chapter might begin: 'The new house was...'. The chapter-break becomes a time-gap, which the reader will imaginatively fill, without the author having to say anything. The impression of passing time is then not destroyed by being compressed into a sentence nor is the narrative delayed. If tedium, or any other mental state, is an important part of that missing period, the character has only to say so later on. The same technique may even be employed within a chapter. If you need a pause midway through, write one – with a blank line, if necessary. Your readers, skilled at watching films, will read this as a kind of 'fade-out' on the page and accept a jump in time or even change of scene quite happily.

KEEPING THE PLOT ALIVE

Jumping between incidents in this way, whether at a chapter-break or not, is one way of keeping all the strands of the plot alive. This

Study Box – Techniques in Practice

In the first extract, the author has avoided the continuous use of 'had' by switching the narrative half-way through into the simple past. (The text could have read 'had had to be taken', 'had elicited', 'had only been able' and 'had shouted'. What effect would these changes have on the passage?)

> The shock to the vet had been so extreme that all three had to be taken to the Buscott Cottage Hospital for treatment. Here the vet's hysterical statement that he objected to blood sports and murdering dwarves wasn't part of his job elicited little sympathy, while Mr Symonds could only account for Willy's injuries by saying he had offered to lend a hand.
> 'Lend a hand?' shouted the doctor. 'He'll be lucky if he keeps the thing. And what the fuck did that to his nose?'
> Tom Sharpe, *Ancestral Vices*

In the next extract we can see how an author can nowadays 'cut', as in a film, from one scene and mood to another without attempting to link the two. This is a consecutive passage in the book (and the space is an essential part of it).

> *Woolagaroo.* Calliope silently tasted the word. *Devil-devil. Stones for its eyes, just like the old story, she said.*

> It was nothing, of course. But it was a little better quality of nothing than anything else so far.

> 'But since you are an attorney, Mr Ramsey, surely you of all people can understand that we don't give out our performer's home lines or any other private information. That would be unheard of, impossible.' Even as she shot him down the public relations woman's smile did not change.
> Tad Williams, *Otherworld – Vol. 2.*
> *River of Blue Fire*

Compare this with a passage written in 1934, when it was generally felt necessary to write linking passages when moving characters between locations – although even here we are beginning to see a move towards 'snapshot' effects rather than a continuous narrative.

> Days of shadow and exhaustion, salt wind and wet mist, foghorn and the constant groan and creak of straining metal. Then they were clear of it, after the Azores. Awnings were out and passengers moved their chairs to windward. High noon and an even keel: the blue water lapping against the sides of the ship, rippling away behind her to the horizon; gramophones and deck tennis: bright arcs of flying fish.
> Evelyn Waugh, *A Handful of Dust*

need may be a serious issue in a longer book, especially if there are a number of sub-plots to resolve. It is not generally satisfactory simply to rotate between the different elements. It is better to plot-point each of them, as suggested earlier, and integrate them at points of maximum effect. Nevertheless, this may entail quite long periods in the narrative when one of the sub-plots is quiescent. How can one keep it before the reader's mind? One method is to have a linking character, one who is minor in the central plot but has a considerable part in the subsidiary storyline. Simply by having that character appear, however briefly, will be sufficient to prompt the reader's memory. If this is impossible, because of the mechanics of your plot, even the mention of a name will sometimes help.

Location and setting can be used in a similar way. A scene set in a particular locale – whether a deserted hay-barn or an office reception area – will be a reminder of a different scene which took place in the same spot earlier, even if the characters involved have no relationship to nor knowledge of one another. An item connected with events will strengthen the effect: mention in passing a huge, blue vase and the reader will instantly recall the previous scene when someone hid behind that ornament. The fact that these two plot-scenes intersect, without the participants being aware of it, can actually add something to the tension of the plot.

Examine your chapters critically to decide where such strategies are relevant. One technique which some people find helpful involves the use of coloured ink or strands of coloured wool, if you have a kinaesthetic bent. Decide on a colour for each important character or each major strand of plot. Read through the chapters you have written, marking the margin in colour to show where the appropriate character or plot-element occurs, or make a chart of this if you do not wish to mark the manuscript. Any point at which one colour disappears for a protracted period is an indication that some sort of reminder should be introduced. If you are using strands of wool, apply the same principle, but plait the strands: one that is dangling loose needs, literally, to be 'woven in' again.

To take a simple example of this system, look at the original plot points for that Faith story again. The use of the colour method makes it clear that Amanda – presumably red, for her hair – disappears entirely from the centre of the book. In so far as this is an important element, the only 'conflict' that there

Five-Minute Exercise

Attempt the colour-code technique with as much of your novel as you have planned in detail. Are there any moments where a hiatus shows?

really is, this absence is unacceptable. The reader must be actively reminded of the rivalry from time to time, which means some additional Amanda scenes. Indeed, she would be a good candidate for a sub-plot of some kind. The same principle applies in any novel. If you find that one aspect of your plot has not been mentioned for several chapters, consider ways of keeping it before the reader's consciousness. This process will not usually entail inventing an entire sub-plot, as in Amanda's case, although it may occasionally require an extra scene.

BUILDING EMOTIONAL VARIETY INTO YOUR NARRATIVE

The colour-chart technique has another useful application too, a kind of refinement on the high-spot principle. It is clear that moments of high drama may be of different kinds: intense grief, anger, passion or death, to name a few. As points on the emotional scale, they might score at opposite extremes. Yet in a narrative they may not offer quite the degree of contrast which this at first suggests.

Decide which emotions figure in your narrative. Award each of these a colour of its own: choose strong colours for strong emotions, paler ones for moods such as contentment, melancholy and placidity, and include some neutral colour such as tan or grey for background information and transactional exchange. Then, make a rough colour-chart of each chapter as you go, awarding an overall colour to each half-page. This technique enables you to see, at a glance, where there is too much background, too much tranquillity or too much action and emotion all at once. A period of reds, purples, oranges and blacks should probably be relieved with a few pastel tones. Think about each colour as you go, and decide in advance what each means to you, rather than seizing on the first thing that comes to hand. Most people have their own associations, when they examine the question. Also, make sure you have a sufficient range of tones – a large set of fibre-tipped pens works very well.

If you have a visual imagination, think of your narrative as a washing line. Bearing the weight of incidents it may tend to sag. The object of this colour-chart technique is to show you, as it were, where a dramatic scene may be inserted, to act as an additional support.

If you have an audial bent, think of each sub-plot as a musical motif and each emotion as a different instrument. Ensure that your motifs are reprised from time to time, and that the emotional orchestration is varied.

Worksheet Six – Planning Chapters and Overcoming Writer's Block

The process of planning chapters is dealt with in the text, and no additional activity is really necessary. However, there is one related element of writing which it may be useful to touch on here, and that is the question of 'writer's block' – the inability, part-way through a novel, to think of what to write.

It is often assumed this 'writer's block' is the result of insufficient planning, or inexperience, and that knowing exactly what comes next in the story will overcome the difficulty. However, as many successful novelists will tell you, this is not the case. Writer's block can afflict anyone, and at any time, and most writers suffer from it to some extent.

It is true, however, that a strong plan is a necessity. It will not of itself make the problem go away, but it does offer the best materials for solving it. If you are afflicted by a 'block' – which usually occurs about halfway through the novel – try some of the following antidotes.

1. Never finish a writing session at the end of a chapter. Facing a totally blank page the next day is a recipe for inducing writer's block. Write at least the first sentence of the next chapter while you are in the flow. Even if you scrap it entirely the next day, it will give you a start.

2. Some people carry this to the extent of not actually finishing the paragraph, or even the sentence, they were working on. Leaving a few words to complete gives them the 'way in' which is always the solution to overcoming block.

3. Begin every session by revising yesterday's. This may be time-consuming, but it is usually time well spent, although it is important not to overdo the trick. If you have a tendency to revise to the extent that you make no new progress at all (as some new writers do), discipline yourself to revise only the last few paragraphs. Again, this gets you 'back into the flow' and for the most part allows you to write on.

4. If, having tried all of the above, you are still stuck and absolutely cannot move on and write the next scene to your satisfaction, try deliberately writing something else. Sometimes this is merely a question of missing out the scene and coming back to it; sometimes it may require more fundamental change – altering the viewpoint or even the incident that you intend to write. Your block may be an indication of a weakness in your plan or characters, and a very slight shift may overcome it easily.

5. If all else fails, simply write. Even if you do not like a single syllable of what you get on paper and you know beyond doubt that you will have to scrap it all and start again, write on. Give yourself a target of, say, five hundred words and simply force yourself to get them down. It will at least give you something to come back to and correct, when inspiration does come back to you, whereas if you sit and stare at white paper it is easy to get permanently stuck. Many authors actually give up at this point.

6. If, after a few days, you are making no real progress, try going back and working through these worksheets once again. Stop being self-critical and just write anything at all. If possible, relax. Allow your subconscious to 'get on with it' – you can always come back and struggle later on.

7. There is one final method, which some writers swear by. It is radical but it seems to work, provided you don't do it more than once. Put your manuscript away and start planning your next novel. When you get stuck on that, come back to volume one – it always seems easier to think about the plot that you're not working on!

8 STYLE AND TECHNIQUE: CONTROLLING PACE

The style in which the book is written makes it easy for me to read on. It does not drag on at the same old pace, nor gallop so fast that I struggle mentally to keep up with it. I will not be baffled by lots of words I do not know (unless they are explained immediately in the text) nor held up by impenetrable dialect. Errors of usage will not interrupt my imaginative flow.

Reader contract

We have seen how organizing the plot can help to keep the narrative alive. However, there is another important element in creating pace, and that is style – the words in which that narrative is told. Minor modifications to your style can be consciously employed in order to increase or diminish pace. But before we examine techniques for doing this, there are some general questions which should be addressed.

GRAMMATICAL INTEGRITY

The reader has a right to expect grammatical integrity in what you write. This means that your English should be basically correct, unless you are using style for particular effect, a technique we shall look at later. If this is in any way a serious problem for you, then you need more help than this book can provide. There are, however, several avenues you can pursue. Find someone who will read and correct your manuscript, preferably someone with an interest in the field. You may find willing friends to help, but not if they make similar mistakes themselves, are too preoccu-

pied with formal style or are embarrassed to correct – and bear in mind that, unless they are writers too, you probably know more about style and effect than they do, by this time. Or you might find a local English language school and have some private lessons there on how the language works; this may be more productive than a general remedial course in English since dealing with foreign learners demands a working understanding of fundamental grammar, register and punctuation. You will also find some titles in the booklist at the end which may help you to brush up your understanding on your own.

Word-processing programs often include a 'grammar' facility and it may be tempting to resort to this. However, like the spell-check, this device should be treated with some caution. Such a program cannot compute the sense of what is written, only apply a few inflexible rules, and those are usually more applicable to American usage rather than British. The facility may prevent you from accidentally missing out a verb, but unless you are fairly confident in grammar anyway it is likely to confuse you rather than inform.

DEVIATING FROM STRICT CORRECTNESS TO ACHIEVE EFFECT

Once you know what is 'grammatically correct', it is possible to depart from that to create effect. We have already seen that dialogue, for instance, has different rules and that omitted words, contracted forms and irregular constructions may actually be desirable in capturing some registers. Similarly, when writing from a viewpoint character – whether interior monologue or a notional third-person narrative – it is perfectly acceptable to use the language which your character would naturally employ, provided that you steer clear of too much dialect.

This may mean commencing sentences with 'and' or 'but', using contracted forms and cutting down on technical vocabulary, or it may mean the very opposite. For reasons which you will doubtless understand if you have read the information about register, formally correct speech, long sentences and polysyllabic words will suggest a character who is a pompous and well-educated bore. However, remember to treat the technique with caution. One or two elaborate words per utterance and a total lack of contracted or idiomatic forms will do the job quite successfully. Your aim is to create the impression of a boring man, not to bore your own readers in the process.

The same principle can be adapted to any style you choose. Errors of usage suggest an uneducated speaker, an archaic idiom evokes the past, a childish vocabulary and lots of questioning combine to give an impression of someone immature. A city businessman may use shorter sentences, but longer words, than his country counterpart. Of course, before you can attempt to use these strategies for effect, it is important that you can write relaxed, correct and neutral prose, so that you can vary it at will.

However, deliberate third-person viewpoints of this kind require management. Conscious deviation from the norm can easily become contrived or difficult to read. A less obvious, but effective strategy is to vary the idiom and imagery of the speaker, rather than the whole construction of the narrative (*see* the section about figures of speech below). If this is combined with touches of the desired register, the effect can be persuasive. Moving between viewpoint characters then becomes more than simply a device for juggling different elements of plot. It can also be a helpful way of varying and controlling pace and so preventing the narrative from either seeming to move too fast or slowing to a monotonous, plodding crawl.

A WORD ABOUT VERBS

Action always tends to raise the pace and add drive to the narrative and action is almost entirely conveyed by verbs. This does not mean that your characters must act energetically, but a scene which appears to be taking too long can on occasion be rescued by just making someone do something, especially if it is unexpected. If you wish us to see emotion, do not tell us what the character feels, look for an action which expresses it: 'She felt nervous' or 'She stood, twisting her handkerchief between her hands.' The second is clichéd – but which reads 'faster' even though it is the longer sentence here? If you have a long passage of description, try adding a few actions to speed up the narrative pace, even if the actual wordage is increased. The opposite is also true: too much action will speed up a quiet scene, so if you want a mood of reverie, cut down the number of things that people do.

'Static' Verbs

Since action is chiefly conveyed by verbs, it might seem that any verb would speed the pace, but this is not invariably the case. You may have learned that verbs are 'doing' words, but not all are active ones. Some simply describe an on-going state. Look at the sentence, 'John is a doctor and he has a car.' John does not have to 'do' anything to make this true: it simply states the facts although there are two verbs in the sentence ('is' and 'has'). Other verbs relate to purely inward activity, such as thought or actions which involve no physical change from the status quo. Consider the sentence, 'John stood by the door and looked down the drive.' Again there are two verbs, but John does not actually move at all. If this is changed to, 'John stood up...', the difference is evident. Also, if you wish to create the impression of activity, use specific verbs instead of general ones: write 'he strode [walked/ran/shuffled/moved] to the door', rather than 'he went'.

'-ing' Verbs

Verbal forms which end in '-ing' (sometimes called present participles), such as smiling and running, are descriptive rather than active (*see below*), especially when they follow 'is' or 'was', and so do not add pace in the usual way. They tend to paint a picture of a scene in which an action is already taking place, even if this interrupted by another action. This is particularly true of non-movement verbs (*see below*), but even if we say 'she was running' we do not see a change in her activity, as we would do with 'she ran'. Indeed, the is/was verb can sometimes be left out, to form a kind of adjectival clause: 'He saw a blackbird flying over the hedge' (short for 'which was flying...'). This form, again without the is/was verb, may also be used at the beginning of a sentence to indicate a brief action that took place immediately before a longer one, often as a necessary prerequisite: 'Taking the key from his pocket, he unlocked the door.' This is clearly less dynamic than the alternative: 'He took the key from his pocket and unlocked the door.' The technique can be employed to build tension and deliberation into a scene, but should not be overdone since it quickly appears clichéd and repetitive. Note that in this last example the two actions must be done by the same person. 'Flying over the hedge he saw a blackbird' means that 'he' was flying, not the bird. There are also occasions where the -ing form becomes a verbal noun (for instance, 'smoking is bad for you'), but these are rare and mentioned only in the interests of completeness. This usage does not affect the pace.

Passive Verbs

If you have studied English language or any foreign tongue, you may remember the so-called 'passive voice', in which we might write for instance, 'My car has been repaired', rather than 'someone has repaired my car'. We often use this structure formally to indicate that we either do not know who did the action or do not particularly care. We are interested only in the result. Since this form is specifically 'passive' rather than 'active' and no movement is involved, it tends to slow the pace or at least add distance and formality to the prose. The only major exception to this is where the person concerned is, for some reason, unable to do things for himself. A man may be knocked down by a car, taken to hospital, X-rayed, operated on and then released – all in the passive voice. We shall achieve a greater impression of action if we use the active voice – 'a car knocked him down, the ambulance men picked him up', and so on – but this ceases to focus on the victim himself. In cases such as this, the passive voice will push the action on like an active verb.

PUNCTUATION: WHAT IT IS AND WHAT IT IS FOR

Punctuation is another area where basic

competence is required. If you are in any doubt, there are books that will help you with the generally accepted rules. This is more than mere convention: punctuation has an important function in your work. It signals to the reader what the phrasing and intonation of the sentences would be if the words were spoken instead of written down.

A *full stop* signals the end of a statement and a falling tone. A *comma* tells the reader that you have not finished yet, but that a short pause is necessary here, and the intonation should rise rather than fall. If this is a new idea to you, try reading those last two sentences aloud. A *semi-colon*(;) indicates a longer pause, and permits a falling tone. A *colon*(:) connects two ideas on the same subject and of equal weight. *Inverted commas* show a quotation, usually of imaginary speech, and tell the reader that he should mentally hear these words in the speaker's voice. *Question* and *exclamation marks* are self-explanatory. *Brackets* and *dashes* signal parenthesis, from the Greek 'put in beside', meaning that the words within the punctuation are an example or a subsidiary idea and should be 'read' in a lower tone throughout.

It is often a good idea to read your work aloud and work out what the natural intonation is, so that you can punctuate accordingly.

One other punctuation mark deserves a mention here, if only because it is so widely misused. The *apostrophe* (') has two functions: sometimes it marks a missing letter (isn't, won't), and that use is generally well understood. Or it may indicate ownership, in which case it follows the owner and – where this is singular – precedes the letter 's': 'this is the lion's den' (one lion); 'this is the lions' den' (several lions). There used to be a convention that where the owner's name already ended in 's', the additional 's' was dropped, but this is changing now: 'Charles's coat' is generally acceptable (as is 'St James's Park'). Plural nouns that do not end in 's' generally take one to show ownership – 'the men's room'. There is one exception to this rule: the word 'it's' can only mean 'it is'; if you intend to say 'belongs to it', the form is 'its', merely to prevent confusion on the page.

That is all. The modern habit of adding an apostrophe before or after every final 's' is not – as yet – acceptable, although English is a living language and in fifty years or so this stricture may seem hilariously archaic.

ENGLISH AS A STRESS-TIMED LANGUAGE

Whether you make use of viewpoint narrative or not, there is another element of style which it is extremely helpful for a writer to understand. It is called 'stress-timing' and relates to the way syllables in a word or sentence are stressed or emphasized, and it is this which gives English prose its distinctive rhythm.

As a writer, you are very lucky here. English is one of a few languages in the world where the length of time it takes to say a sentence depends, not on how many syllables there are, but how many of those syllables are stressed. (If all this seems a little technical, I apologize, it may be difficult to grasp at first but it is worth persevering with, for the interesting effects it can achieve.)

Look at the following examples: 'He loves you' and 'It's a beautiful day.' How many syllables are there in each? (The answer, in case you have difficulty with this, is that there are three syllables in the first sentences and six in the second – the second is twice as long.) However, if you say the sentences aloud, you will realize that the number of stressed syllables is the same – the first syllable in each case being lightly stressed, followed by two stronger stresses. The intermediate syllables in the second sentence almost disappear, and the vowel sounds become indistinct (technically, they are 'reduced to a medial'). Contrary to some opinion, this is not a fault but part of the uniqueness of the English tongue. The result is that the two sentences, in normal speech, should take exactly the same length of time to say. Try it with a friend and see. In fact, if you watch any politician speak you will find that he nods his head or gestures with his hand exactly in time with the stresses of the syllables he speaks. English speakers do not usually wave their hands around as speakers of other languages are apt to do; we naturally gesticulate in time with the intrinsic rhythm of our syllables, and those stresses fall at more or less regular intervals, which is what stress-timing means.

This is obviously of interest to a poet, since it is the basis of all English rhythm, but it does have importance for the writer of fiction too, because the number and frequency of stressed syllables in a sentence materially affects its apparent pace. Or, to put that another way, many quick stresses make the words seem sharp. (If you are in any doubt about this fact, look at those last two sentences again, and notice what happens to the stress.) This is why so many writing courses urge that long words and long sentences slow down the pace. They do, quite literally. If you understand the reason for this, it will be easier for you not merely to avoid the problem but to use this knowledge for deliberate effect. It is clear that long words necessarily have more intermediate, unstressed syllables. Long sentences do too. Short words and short sentences have the opposite effect. We have already noted that the first word of any sentence has a mini-stress, so a long sentence may actually have fewer stresses than the same words separated into two sentences. (Look at this sentence and see what happens if you divide it into two.)

Obviously, therefore, if you are writing an action scene it makes sense to ensure that your sentences are short. If you are writing a romantic idyll, on the other hand, or a passage of poetically descriptive prose, longer words and sentences will help to set a more reflective pace. Once again, treat this technique with caution: the idea is to slow the pace, not bring it to a halt. In any case, do not overdo the trick. If the reader spots what you are doing, it will seem contrived.

One final word about stress-timed effects: every native English speaker has a natural rhythm of his or her own, to which written as well as spoken sentences will instinctively conform. When writing long passages of narrative, one can consciously vary the length of sentences and substitute a longer or a shorter word sometimes. In that way the style does not become monotonous in pace. If you are writing dialogue, in particular, it is a useful discipline to interfere deliberately with the rhythm of your sentences from time to time, so that your characters do not always share your voice. If you become skilled at this, you may be able to create a distinctive rhythm for your major characters, which is a good way of distinguishing between them.

AN AUTHOR'S ARMOURY OF PACE CONTROL

There are a number of specific stylistic elements which affect pace. Here, for easy memory, are the major ones. The ten most important devices which speed pace may be called for convenience p-a-c-e-m-a-k-e-r-s.

P is for *Punchiness*
This is the simplest way of adding pace. Short, punchy words and sentences speed up the pace. So do short paragraphs. For moments of really high tension try a combination of the three – a short, single-sentence paragraph. There is a practical element in this. Short words, sentences and paragraphs make a page of print look much less dense than longer

93

ones, and obviously, where there is a lot of space, the page will physically take less time to read. If you are writing a dramatic scene and find that the sentences and paragraphs are all fairly long, try the simple expedient of cutting them in half.

A is for *Action*

See under Verbs above. Dialogue is a kind of action, too, since the characters are 'doing something' – speaking, in this case (*see also* Chapter 5). A piece of narrative may be speeded up by having a character 'say' the words, instead of the author doing so direct. 'She suddenly decided to go out', can become '"I'm going out!", she said, suddenly.' Remember, however, that, although complex construction may sometimes echo character, it will slow the pace as much in dialogue as elsewhere.

C is for *Changes*

Variety of mood, tone, incident, character, setting and even pace itself will keep the reader persisting to the end. Even an action story requires some moments of tranquillity; a more poetic story needs some action now and then.

E is for *Excitement*

The things which add excitement to real life – love, danger, risk, happiness, surprise – will add pace and excitement to your narrative.

M is for *Movement*

If a passage is becoming 'stuck', move somebody or something energetically. Sometimes moving the paragraph itself may be the solution to the problem. Note that since speaking does not involve much physical activity, long passages of dialogue require some movement by the characters to maintain the pace.

A is for *Anticipation*

This can be achieved within a scene by having a character break off halfway through a significant sentence – and it must be significant to achieve effect – for instance, when the reader is expecting some revelation, confession or a declaration of love. Or you may break off a chapter just before an expected high point and switch the scene to something or to someone else. Leaving the reader waiting for some confrontation which is clearly inevitable, but that the characters do not know about can also add pace. This technique should be used sparingly, however, or it irritates. Save it for moments important to the plot.

K is for *Killing*

(Rather a cheat, this, but an effective trick.) One sure way of keeping up the tension and the pace is to have a death, not necessarily of a high-level character nor even of a person at all. Any death – a horse, a cat run over by a car, even the deliberate murder of a fly – will do.

E is for *Enthusiasm*

Your own enthusiasm and interest are essential. If you are bored or uninterested in a character or scene it will inevitably show through in plodding prose. If this happens, it is probably best to scrap that part of the narrative or find some other way of managing that element of plot.

R is for *Repetition*

Repeating the same short word or phrase or the same sentence structure in a short space of time always has a dramatic effect upon the pace because of the stress patterns involved (*see above*). The degree to which it speeds the prose generally depends upon the length of the word or sentence repeated: 'Damn! Damn! Damn!', for instance, or: 'Not in the shower. Not on the balcony. Not in the hall.' Because this is such a potent technique it is important to make sure that you do not repeat things by mistake and so accidentally influence the pace. It is easy to overuse a favourite sentence construction without being aware of it. This is also why many writing courses advise you to avoid recurring words and try to find synonyms instead.

S is for *Surprise*

This is always an important element, at every level in the narrative. Avoid clichés, such as 'packed together like sardines', and try to produce a fresher, more surprising image of your own. That same scene might be 'packed as a rush-hour tube' to a city character, while a farm-worker viewpoint might describe the crowd as 'jostled together like a herd of cows'.

In the same way, make your adjectives and adverbs add something to your prose; there is nothing surprising about a 'small kitten' or a 'snarling tiger', but a 'snarling kitten' may be memorable. The same principle is also true of plot. Even when the ultimate outcome is predictable, as in a conventional romance, try to find some element of surprise along the way to keep your reader interested and your pace alive.

If *p-a-c-e-m-a-k-e-r-s* increase the speed, it follows that the opposite techniques will slow it down. Of course, sometimes this may be what you want, part of the overall variety. Figures of speech, for instance, because they often express reality through allusion rather

---

Study Box

Here are two examples of how technical devices can create effect. Hardy uses a combination of repeated syntax, together with the use of detail – a slowing-down device – to create an amusing picture of Dick's state of mind while Fancy keeps him waiting as she sews: King, in a wholly different vein, uses repetition and short sentences to create an atmosphere of menace.

> The clock struck three. Dick arose from his seat, walked around the room with his hands behind him, examining all the furniture, then sounded a few notes on the harmonium, then looked inside all the books he could find, then smoothed Fancy's head with his hand. Still the snipping and sewing went on.
> The clock struck four. Dick fidgeted about, yawned privately: counted the knots in the table: yawned publicly: counted the flies on the ceiling, yawned horribly; went into the kitchen and

scullery and so thoroughly studied the principle upon which the pump was constructed that he could have delivered a lecture on the subject. . . . The clock struck five and still the snipping and sewing went on.

Thomas Hardy,
Under the Greenwood Tree

> Louder. Louder.
> There was a tiger in the hall, and now the tiger was just around the corner, still crying out in that shrill and petulant and lunatic rage, the rogue mallet slamming, because this tiger walked on two legs and was –
> He woke with a sudden indrawn gasp, sitting bolt upright in bed, his eyes wide and staring into the darkness, hands crossed in front of his face.
> Something on one hand. Crawling.
> Wasps. Three of them.

Stephen King, *The Shining*

than 'punchily' can create a more dreamy and poetic mood, and so on throughout the entire ten elements. However, there are some habits which are dangerous, because they do not merely slow the pace, they can actually constitute a *s-l-u-m-p*.

S is for *Static*
Scenes where nobody moves at all, where there is nothing but description or background or where only internal thoughts and dialogue take place. (Remember that flashbacks using 'had' come into this category, because there is no action happening in the 'present' time.)

L is for *Length*
Beware of long passages using long words, long sentences and long paragraphs.

U is for *Undigested Research*
Because material has been researched that does not mean it must automatically be included in the book. If a piece of fascinating background does not fit seamlessly into your narrative, leave it out. Avoid writing researched information as a block – undigested research can quickly slow the narrative to a crawl – and never be tempted to write a scene or chapter simply to incorporate some stray fact not related to the plot.

M is for *Mathematical Minutiae*
Statistics of almost any kind are dangerous, and unnecessary detail always decelerates the pace. If a lot of detail is essential to your plot (perhaps for historical or lyrical effect) ensure that you incorporate other techniques to keep the pace alive, and do not give uninterrupted detail unless, as in a mystery or detective plot, you actively wish the reader to skim over it.

P is for *Plodding, Padding* and *Predictability*
These three can be the death of pace.

Finally, here are five extracts, all of which illustrate in some way techniques which we have looked at in this book. They are offered this time without comment, so that you can analyse them for yourself. (The first two extracts are opening paragraphs, and no excuse is made for the length of the Roddy Doyle quotation, which needs to be read in its entirety.)

There must be better ways, Jason Bradley kept telling himself, of celebrating one's twenty-first birthday than attending a mass funeral: but at least he had no emotional involvement. He wondered if Operation JENNIFER's Director, or his CIA sidekicks, even knew the names of the sixty-three Russian sailors they were now consigning to the deep.

Arthur C. Clarke,
The Ghost from the Grand Banks

Lessa woke, cold. Cold with more than the chill of the everlastingly clammy stone walls. Cold with the prescience of danger stronger than the one ten full Turns ago that had then sent her, whimpering with terror, to hide in the watch-wher's odorous lair.

Anne McCaffrey, *Dragonflight*

'He'll not catch Mr Crowther napping,' Mrs Watty observed. 'Mr Crowther is very quick at the repartee.'

Flora asked, 'Who's Mr Crowther?'

'He's the Presbyterian meenister,' Anthony told her, in an accent more Highland than Mrs Watty's own.

Jason chipped in, 'And Mrs Crowther teaches Sunday School, and she's got very big teeth.'

Rosamunde Pilcher, *Under Gemini*

- Is your homework done?
- Yes.

- All of it?
- Yes.
- The learning?
- Yes.
- What did you get?
- Ten spellings.
- Ten of them: give us one?
- Sediment. Do you want me to do it?
- There's no point, but yeah.
- S.e.d.i.m.e.n.t.
- Sediment.
- C.e.n.t.e.n.a.r.y.
- Centenary.
- Yeah. That's the name for a hundredth anniversary.
- Like your mother's birthday.

I'd done it. It was alright. Normal again. He'd cracked a joke. Ma had laughed. I'd laughed. He'd laughed. Mine lasted longest. During it, I thought it was going to change into a cry. But it didn't. My eyes blinked like mad and then it was okay.

- Sediment has three syllables, I told them.

Roddy Doyle *Paddy Clarke ha ha ha*

'You can't turn something into something else,' said Corporal Nobbs. 'The Alchemists have been trying it for years.'

'They can gen'rally turn a house into a hole in the ground,' said Sergeant Colon.

'That's what I'm talking about,' said Corporal Nobbs. 'Can't be done. It's all to do with ... elements. An alchemist told me. Everything's made up of elements, right? Earth, Water, Air, Fire and ... sunnick. Well known fact. Everything's got them all mixed up just right.'

He stamped his feet in an effort to get some warmth into them.

Terry Pratchett, *The Truth*

9 PREPARING A MANUSCRIPT

In order to sell your manuscript, it is usual to submit a proposal package to a publisher or an agent. This consists of three parts: a covering letter, a synopsis (or outline) of your story and a small number of specimen chapters (usually the first three). This proposal is very important. It is your flagship. This is the moment at which you may sell your book. It is important to understand this. Many writers believe that the 'real' book is the manuscript which is lurking on the study table. In fact, this is far from the truth. A book rarely represents the typescript that was originally submitted. Almost all first-time writers need to revise, sometimes substantially, at the editing stage. However, what 'sold' the idea was the proposal package. Once the publisher is committed to that, an editor will guide you as to the rest. It is important, therefore, that your proposal gives the best possible impression of your intended book. Let us examine the three parts of it in detail.

THE COVERING LETTER

This is the first thing that an editor will see, so make sure that it looks professional. Simply point out that you are enclosing a novel for his attention: give a very brief idea about the nature, the setting and the length of your novel, and any information about your own writing career – if you have had anything professionally published, for example, or particular reasons why you are especially qualified to write on this topic. If you are writing a 'police procedural' and you used to be a member of the force, or you have made a special study of medieval France, which is the setting for your novel, then say so. Nothing else. Keep it short and utterly businesslike. Do not tell the editor what a wonderful publishing house it is nor how your mother always buys their imprint nor how you are sure that this manuscript is just what they are wanting because your Auntie Flo liked it. This letter is only there to make a swift, personal link between yourself and the editor, and the real message is 'I am not a total amateur'. Do not let the letter give a different impression.

The opening of a covering letter might read something like this:

> I enclose a synopsis and the first three chapters of a short (30,000-word) novel with the working title *Moonlight on Malta*. It is a short, contemporary romance set in Malta, as the title suggests, against the background of industrial espionage in the perfume industry. I believe it is similar in general style to other titles you have published and wonder whether you would be good enough to consider it for your list. I enclose an SAE.

This letter tells the editor:

- the genre (light contemporary romance)
- the length and the working title
- the setting
- the background and potential conflict

- that you have researched the market and selected this publisher, not stuck a pin into the *Writers' and Artists' Yearbook*
- that you have enclosed return postage (most important if you ever hope to see your precious manuscript again).

THE SYNOPSIS

The synopsis requires special care; it is not merely an outline of the book in a way that a non-fiction proposal might be. The object is to make the book as exciting as possible, so devote a little time to style even in the synopsis that you send. It should include:

- a thumbnail sketch of the major characters – not their physical descriptions but their personalities, motives and the things they care about
- an indication of the setting – geographical, historical, commercial or artistic
- an indication of the themes and conflicts in the novel
- last, but not least, an indication of the major events of the narrative; use your plot points as the basis for the summary and do not try to flesh them out too much, two or three pages is the maximum so there is no room for a highly detailed account – spelling out every tiny twist and turn will only make your submission look amateurish.

Write with good, bold strokes to try to make the book sound interesting, so that the editor wants to read not only the chapters you enclose but the remainder of the manuscript as well. That, after all, is the effect you are looking for. If you can write this well enough, you not only convince the publishers of your competence, but they may even use part of your own synopsis as the cover blurb.

So the *Moonlight* synopsis might begin something like this:

FAITH (young, intelligent, but inexperienced and a bit nervous) is sent to Malta at short notice to represent her company Moonlight Cosmetics in a meeting with the wealthy and glamorous French importer JEAN-PIERRE LAVAL. At the airport, however, she is stranded and is offered a lift by a stranger, the dashing but mysterious HANNIBAL, a time-share agent who appears to have strangely accurate information about Faith and her visit. Jean-Pierre warns her against the younger man, but he, in his turn, warns her that there is something sinister about the Laval commercial empire. As the visit goes on, more and more troubling events occur. Someone tampers with her suitcase; she is followed by a mysterious man in a red cap; she discovers that Hannibal was once employed by Laval.

And so on. Give a proper overview of the whole novel and a clear picture of what the main events will be. Make sure that you sketch in the resolution too (despite what you may read in some older manuals) since publishers – particularly where previously unpublished writers are concerned – need to know that you have thought through the plot and that you can sustain the narrative until the end. Look at the section on creating plot-points again and ensure that your links in the chain are sufficiently strong to support the story to the end. Do not try to skip this or bluff your way with generalities. To an experienced eye, an inadequate plan will betray itself at once.

SAMPLE CHAPTERS

These are the first three chapters of the novel. It is essential that they show what you can do and they should be designed to keep the reader turning the pages and reading on. Pay particular attention to style before you send them off: look at the section in this book on style and pace and make the sample chapters as good as you can. If you interest the editor with these, you will stand a good chance of selling the whole book.

It has been said before, but pay particular attention to the following:

1. Vary the length of paragraphs. Ensure that there is good variation and that all paragraphs are not all more or less of the same length. The fact of even-spacing paragraphs alone can influence the pace of a manuscript, making it boring to read, however lively the style.

2. Keep sentences and vocabulary short unless there is a good reason for doing otherwise. The arbitrary selection of a polysyllabic vocabulary in preference to a colloquial lexis can be an obfuscating and distancing stylistic practice. Or, to put it another way, do not use long, complex words and sentences when short and simple ones will do. Try to use a vivid, lively vocabulary and a variety of sentence structures. Think about your reader and do not make him struggle to follow you, or bore him half to death with dusty and repetitive prose.

3. Apply your 'pacemaker' techniques carefully to these chapters: work for confrontation, dialogue and action, and try to steer away from any 'slump' effects.

4. Try to leave your characters, at the end of your sample chapters, at dramatic moments or with the introduction of threats or intrigues; use your plot points to help you to select what those moments are, even if this means adapting your original plan a little, and ensure that you end at an interesting point. The idea is to leave your editor wanting to read on.

WHAT ABOUT A TITLE?

You will have noticed that earlier in this chapter the term 'working title' was used. This is deliberate. Of course, the ideal title may occur to you, but finding an appropriate one can be difficult, and, even if you think that you have found one, your publisher or editor might not agree, because of house style, marketing or just because there are too many other, similar titles on the shelves. There is no need to be disturbed by this. Apart from titles already in the bookshops, the publisher will have new ones in production and there are so many published every month that it is hard to be truly original.

On the other hand, you have probably mentally called your story something all along, and it is perfectly acceptable to submit a manuscript under a working title. Many authors do. You may not be entirely pleased with it, but even a working title should give an impression of the manuscript, and it is worth taking a little time and effort over this. Try to choose a title that is fairly short, gives some indication of the genre and mood, and is eye-catching. Imagine your book on a bookseller's shelf, merely one of the hundreds of titles there. What will make a reader select your book from the many?

Do bear in mind, however, that the final choice of title lies with your editor, and your original suggestion may be changed. Similarly, you may have little say, if any, over the jacket illustration. This is a sore point with authors, especially if your raven-haired beauty is represented on the cover as a diminutive blonde. By that time, though, you have sold your novel and the real battle has been won.

LOOK PROFESSIONAL

It should be hardly necessary in the twenty-first century to urge that your submission should be typed, on one side of good quality, white, A4 paper, using double spacing. Leave space at the top and the bottom of each sheet and generous margins at both sides, usually a little wider on the left than on the right. This is not merely for ease of reading, but because this is where the printer's symbols will go. Even if there were no alterations to the text, which is unlikely, there would still be instructions to the printer about spacing, capitals, indentation and the like in accordance with the publisher's house style. A sensible margin is around 40mm on the left and 25–30mm on the right.

There are no strict rules about the layout of a manuscript, and different authorities give different advice. Some writing schools suggesting putting the 'strap' (title, author's name and page-number) at the top right-hand side of each page, others favour placing it at the bottom left. On the whole, probably any clear, professional layout will do. Nevertheless, the emphasis is on *professional*, and there are some conventions which you should observe. The title page should show:

1. The title of the book.

2. The author's name.

3. An indication of the number of words in the manuscript.

4. Your full name (if different) and address, including post-code and telephone number. Some manuals suggest including a copyright claim here too, but this is not necessary; if you do include one, make it as discreet as possible. The law says that your own work remains your copyright the moment that you have committed it to paper, claims that you have 'lodged a copy with your lawyer' will only make you look like an amateur. No publisher nor editor is going to steal your idea and, in any case, story-ideas are not copyright, only

the actual words in which they are couched. Given the huge numbers of manuscripts about, it would be amazing if someone had not had a similar idea.

5. For a proposal package, it is also a good idea to indicate how many pages or chapters are enclosed, so that if any go missing this is obvious; hence, I might create a title page as shown overleaf.

6. Begin page 1 of Chapter 1 on a new page, with the title and chapter heading (if any) clearly displayed. I have seen it suggested that authors should leave a large gap after the title line and begin the typescript halfway down the page – for the first chapter only – but that is not strictly necessary; I have never done so myself nor been invited to.

7. Either at the bottom or the top of every page, include the ' strap', as mentioned earlier. This does not have to include the full title where that is long, so our *Moonlight* story might have a strap like this: Moonlight: Lacey, p. 3

8. Some authorities suggest that you add 'm/f', meaning 'more follows', to the end of every page but the last. I have not found this strictly necessary with novels, though it is indispensable with shorter manuscripts such as short stories. However, it does indicate that there are further pages, so it is an additional insurance for your manuscript. Type 'm/f' at the bottom of your page, if you choose to use it, even if the rest of your strap appears at the top. When you come to the last page, substitute the word 'ends' for 'm/f'. Do not embellish your manuscript by typing THE END across the middle of the paper and underlining it.

9. Pages should be numbered from page 1 of Chapter 1 in numerical sequence until the end

Moonlight on Malta
by
Brenda Lacey
(approx. 50,000 words)
First three chapters only – synopsis enclosed

Your name,
3 Any Street,
Any town
Someshire PC1 W23
Tel. 0123 456789
Copyright: B. Lacey 2003

of the book. Do not begin numbering again for each chapter, nor even for each section, where that applies. If you are using a typewriter, rather than a word-processor or computer, and you find that you have missed numbering a page, do not alter all the numbers to the end of the manuscript but insert it. For instance, if you missed numbering page 18, put it in its proper place (between 17 and the misnumbered 18, which should have been 19) and mark it page 17A, or Folio 17A (pages in an manuscript are properly called ' folios'). To make quite sure that the editor knows what you are doing, you may add 'Insert Folio 17A here' on the bottom of page 17. Conversely, if you miss out a page number, mark this on the page before. So, if you went from 27 to 29 by accident, you might write 'Go to Folio 29' at the bottom of page 27, or simply number that one as 27/28.

10. There was a convention for a time that only complete paragraphs should appear on any given page of manuscript, but that is no longer necessary. However, it is a good idea to avoid what are called in the trade 'widows and orphans' – single lines beginning a paragraph at the bottom of a page or single lines ending one at the beginning of the next. In other words, having only one line of a longer paragraph on any one page. If you have a computer or word-processor, it will probably be set to avoid this automatically or at least can be instructed to do so; if you still use a typewriter, you will have to take account of this for yourself.

11. A word about paragraphs: I was taught to indent them, and still do when writing fiction, and nobody has yet complained. The modern American habit of starting all paragraphs at

the right-hand margin has not yet generally caught on in the publishing world, although some do like to begin the first paragraph of each chapter in this fashion. Details like this seem to vary from publisher to publisher, and there is no need to worry about them too much at the submission stage. One of my editors routinely changes my (British) spelling of words such as 'realize' and 'visualize' to the American 'realise' and 'visualise'; another publishing house requires the British form. Differences of this kind make up house style, and when your manuscript has been accepted, your editor will let you know what your particular publisher requires.

12. Read through your manuscript and make sure that it is as correct as possible. In particular, if you are using a spell-check facility ensure that the final manuscript makes sense – a spell-check will pick up only misprints that are not real words; it is not able to decide whether the real word is the one the author meant. Sentences such as 'she lifted her tea-stained face to his' are hilarious, but get through the spell-check without difficulty.

13. You do not have to count every word in your text to arrive at the approximate word-count on the title. The traditional method for doing this is to take a random sample of the number of words in sections of six complete lines from different pages, and then take an average. Then take another random sample of six pages and calculate the average number of lines per page (with computers this is easy, since they will be set to the same number of lines on every page). Multiply that by the number of pages in your manuscript, and you have the approximate total that you need.

These days word-processing programs have an automatic word-count facility, but you will find that this yields a different result from the manual method since it computes the number of words in a completely different way. If you are using this method of arriving at your word-count, make this explicit on the title page, or better still, work out your total in the non-electronic way as well and include both results, remembering to indicate which is which, of course.

Whichever method you adopt, you will need put the total on the cover page, so you obviously need to count up first and type up your title page last of all.

14. If your manuscript will fit into a single plastic file, well and good, and your proposal package may well do so. Otherwise put the pages loose into a wallet file – the type that folds over, to prevent the pages from falling out – or into the cardboard box your typing paper came in and send it off in that. Do not punch holes in your manuscript or try to staple it together. Do not put separate chapters into separate plastic files and submit the whole thing in a lever-file nor fasten sheets together with pins or bull-dog clips. If the text will not fit into an A4 envelope, invest in a good-sized Jiffy bag and enclose a return postage slip instead of an SAE. Then, post it off and get on with writing something else.

YOU HAVE SENT YOUR MANUSCRIPT... WHAT HAPPENS NEXT?

Commission

You may be lucky and be commissioned straightaway to write the novel on the basis of your proposal. A more likely step to success is that the publisher/agent will not commit himself, but will ask to see the completed manuscript. Do note that your original synopsis is not absolutely binding at this stage. The publisher himself may suggest changes in the way you have organized the material or propose that you give some incident or character much greater prominence. In the same way, if you suddenly decide that you want to include some fascinating new development, your editor will usually permit it, providing that the integrity of the story remains. However, this does not suggest that it is feasible to make wholesale changes in the original. When you submit your outline, you are offering the basis for a contract, in the same way that a dressmaker might submit designs to a client. You may slightly tailor the original to fit your customer's specification or add a decorative detail or two of your own, but you cannot submit designs for a ball-gown and then produce a battledress and expect that to be acceptable.

Correcting Proofs

If your manuscript is accepted, it will probably not be printed as it stands. First, your editor may want changes – sometimes even substantial changes – in the text, and the manuscript will certainly be 'sub-edited', meaning that little infelicities of expression will be pointed out, ambiguities resolved, and changes quite possibly made to punctuation. Significant changes are always discussed with the author, and you will usually be able to see the manuscript before it goes to be typeset.

Even at that point your work is not complete. You will eventually have typesetter's proofs to look at and to correct. Please note that 'correct' is the important word. This is not an opportunity to rewrite the book. Of course, if there are important errors or omissions which you yourself have made, and which you only spot at this juncture, they must certainly be changed. The editor will also usually permit you to alter a word or two in the interests of style, provided that the changes do not have knock-on effects for pages afterwards. But these changes should be minimal, and wholesale revisions are unacceptable – adding a paragraph can require half a chapter to be

renumbered and reset. Some publishers will charge you for the cost if you wish to incorporate more than a minimum amount of change.

You are supposed to be looking for *errors*, where the typescript does not match the submitted script – omissions, misspellings, punctuation, spacing and other errors of that kind. There are conventional signs to indicate the kind of error made, one inserted at the error in the text, and the other in the margin at the side, to draw the editor's attention to the line. You will find a full list of them in the *Writers' and Artists' Yearbook*, together with clear instructions for how to mark the text. Most publishers prefer you to mark up your proofs in either red or green ink, to provide a clear contrast with the black print.

Be prepared to read the script through several times. It is easy to read what you expect to see and not what is actually on the page. You may it find it helpful to read twice from the front, to ensure that the sense is correct, and then once backwards from the bottom of the page, so that you are looking at the punctuation and the spelling of the words. Correct your proofs and send them back.

While you are correcting your set of proofs, a sub-editor will be doing the same with another copy. The two will be collated, and the book then goes to print. You should get a few copies for your own use, and you are usually able to buy additional ones at a substantial discount. You do *not* get large piles of free copies, whatever your friends and relatives may think, so be prepared. (Your contract will have spelled all this out for you.) There are, however, few joys to compare with the delight of seeing your first novel in print, with your name on it.

Rejection

It has to be faced, your work may be met by a rejection letter. Sometimes this is an outright rejection, sometimes a letter which will identify for you why the material has not been accepted, in which case take it to heart. It may be that you really cannot accept the advice given, but do not simply reject it out of hand. Any editor who takes the time to write you a letter such as this is, in fact, paying you a compliment and offering you guidance about how best to succeed, though it is sometimes hard to see it in this way. This is especially true today, when most publishers and agents are overwhelmed with submitted manuscripts, and anything other than a printed rejection slip is now the exception rather than the rule. So if you get a constructive letter, be pleased rather than disappointed and try to learn from it.

Rejection may even occur after the editor has asked for a full manuscript – it has happened to me. In that case, send it out again. (Mine was published in the end.) We all of us have something to learn from the well-known writer who tells the story of how she got her first book published after submitting it to fifteen different publishers and reworking it fifteen times. She went on to be a bestseller. And the message is not that she went on to be a bestseller, but that she went on sending and reworking the material. Most of us would have given up long before.

'Yes, but...' Letters

Even if your manuscript is accepted, it does not follow that your work on it is finished. The editor may want substantial changes to be made, and, if you are wise, you will accede politely, if not eagerly, to any such suggestions. There may be several reasons why revisions may be required. There may be straightforward changes to improve the style or pace, or there may be more far-reaching suggestions for expanding or (more usually) omitting certain characters, descriptions or incidents – often passages of which you were yourself particularly fond. There is a saying in the writing world, 'murder your darlings' – if you think a certain passage is particularly apt and charming, cut it out at once. Or as Samuel Johnson's Oxford tutor said to him, 'Read over your compositions, and wherever you meet with a passage which you think is particularly fine, strike it out.' It is wise to accept advice on this, at least with your first novel. Your editor knows the market: you do not. If you feel very strongly about this, explain why. It may be that he or she knows something which you do not.

On the other hand, there may be changes suggested for completely arbitrary reasons – the number of pages or the house format for novels of this kind. Even if you have done your homework carefully, you might find yourself the victim of this. Editors change, and so does editorial policy and fashion. This may seem irritating, but remember, it is the publisher's money which is finally at stake, and he who pays the piper has the right to call the tune.

THE CASE FOR WORD-PROCESSORS

If you can afford one, a word-processor or computer is an invaluable tool. Because the text comes up on a screen before you print, you are able to correct it endlessly until it reads exactly as you wish. You can move paragraphs around, try different versions of sentences, even change the name of a character throughout, and, as has already been observed, the machine will number pages, check spelling and ensure that your format is consistent.

Do, however, ensure that you remember to save a copy of your work in a specific file location or on a separate disk. Most machines can now be set to 'save' every half hour or at some other interval automatically, and this will prevent the dreadful heartbreak of having

105

some email virus, technical breakdown, electric storm or other catastrophe wiping out your entire manuscript. I even find it advisable to print a hard copy every now and then, especially as I am unable to see mistakes and misprints on the screen as effectively as I can see them in print.

If you are accustomed to a typewriter or, even more, to writing a literal 'manuscript' by hand, you may find the technology onerous at first. However, in the twenty-first century it is fast becoming an essential tool. Publishers increasingly request a copy and a disc, instead of several printed copies of the text, and this practice is likely to increase as time goes on.

SHOULD I HAVE AN AGENT?

This is a question which I am often asked, and my reply would be, 'Of course – if you can find one.' I was lucky, a publishing house passed my name to an agent and I would be lost without her. You can find the names of agents through the *Writers' and Artists' Yearbook* or the Macmillan *Writer's Handbook*, or any of the writers' magazines. If you can find a new agent who is starting out alone, he (or she) will be seeking to build up a list and may be more likely to take on an unknown name. However, the method of approach is exactly the same as that for approaching a publisher direct – by sending in a proposal.

Once you have found an agent, you are spared the personal anguish of handling your rejections, choosing the most likely publisher, trying to bargain for the most favourable terms or exploiting the additional contract 'rights'. Your agent will do all this for you, in return for a percentage of what you earn. Whether you decide to try and find an agent or a publisher first is entirely up to you. Finding the one is nearly as difficult as obtaining the other. Some writing schools suggest trying to get a publisher interested first, as an agent is obviously more likely to look kindly on someone with a contract in view, although a commission on your earnings would still be required.

BUSINESS MATTERS

One final point: money which you receive from royalties is INCOME, and as such must be declared to the Inland Revenue. There is no point in overlooking this, publishers submit a detailed statement of their outgoings.

It is wise to keep a notebook, and, when you send anything off, make a note of the publisher to whom you submitted it and the date. If it is rejected, make a note of the date that it came back, and start the process again. When it is accepted, note the date of your contract and, similarly, when and how much you were paid. Make a note of your outgoings as well, because these may be set against tax when you start to earn. Postage, stationery, printer ribbons and computer repairs, attendance at writers' courses and conferences and even subscriptions to authors' organizations can all be claimed for in this way.

If you propose to purchase a computer and printer you can seek advice about claiming a proportion of the cost as capital expenses (and, naturally, there are programs which will help you keep personal financial records). Once you have sold a book, you may be able to claim tax relief on such items as the costs of genuine research, although the law on this is complex and it is wise to take advice. There are a number of publications from the Inland Revenue and elsewhere which will give you information, or you may prefer to employ an accountant, as I do, to ensure that your advice is up to date.

Lastly, if you earn more than a given sum from your writing, you will have to register for VAT; at the time of writing (early 2003) the threshold is about £40,000 per annum, but the level goes up from time to time; Customs and Excise will advise. However, when you are earning on that scale, an expert accountant is advisable – and by that time you will hardly need this book.

FINALLY... TEN WAYS TO GET REJECTED

Here is a checklist which I developed many years ago for members of my postal writing course:

- *Reinvent the wheel:* tell the same story someone else has told
- *Explain your characters:* never let them disclose their personality
- *Just base your story on real incidents:* do not edit nor invent
- *Ensure that every sentence is grammatical:* even dialogue
- *Commence at the beginning:* tell the reader all the background first
- *Tell the reader everything you know:* do not waste good research
- *Include plenty of conversation:* exactly as you hear it every day
- *Offer adjectives and adverbs everywhere:* description is good
- *Never deviate from your natural pace and style and*
- *Send it to the first publisher you think of.*

Read these 'rules' again and be sure that you understand why doing these things would be counterproductive. (Read the initial letters in each case!) On the other hand, I am afraid that there is only one certain way to avoid rejection for your manuscript: put it in the bottom drawer and do not send it anywhere.

However, if you apply the ideas and techniques in this book, you should give yourself a better chance. If you are at first rejected, do not despair. Every book on how to write will tell you this, but it is true. Selecting anything for publication is a subjective choice – do you like every book your neighbour likes? So, treat any advice they give you as a compliment, they would not bother if they did not like it at all – send a nice, clean text off to someone else, and get started on your second book. Good luck!

FURTHER READING

IMAGINATIVE STYLE

Baddeley, A.D., *Human Memory: Theory and Practice* (Psychology Press, 1997)
Cytowic, R., *The Man Who Tasted Shapes* (Abacus, 1994)
Gardner, H., *Frames of Mind: The Theory of Multiple Intelligence* (Basic Books, 1993)
Motluk, Roche, Cytowic, *et al.*, 'Sweet Smell of Purple' (series of papers published in *New Scientist*, Aug. 1994 *et seq.*)

REGISTER

Joos, M., *English Form and Meaning* (University of Wisconsin, 1964)
Joos, M., *The Five Clocks* (Penguin, 1967)
Myers-Scotton, C. (ed.), *Codes and Consequences: Choosing Linguistic Varieties* (Oxford University Press, 1998)

GRAMMAR, USAGE AND PUNCTUATION

Crystal, D., *Rediscover Grammar* (Longman, 1998)
Leech and Svartvic, *A Communicative Grammar of English* (Longman, 1994)
Pinker, S., *Words and Rules, The Ingredients of Language* (Phoenix, 2000)
Trask, E., *The Penguin Guide to Punctuation* (Penguin, 1997)

GENERAL

Blake, C., *From Pitch to Publication* (Pan, 1999)
Braine, J., *Writing a Novel* (Eyre Methuen, 1974)
Brande, D., *Becoming a Writer* (Macmillan, 1983)
Highsmith, P., *Plotting and Writing Suspense Fiction* (St. Martin's Press, 2001)
Jute, A., *Writing a Thriller* (A. & C. Black, 1994)
Jute, A., *Writing Proposals and Synopses that Sell* (Thomas and Lochar, 1998)
Legat, M., *Writing for Profit and Pleasure* (Robert Hale, 1995)
Lodge, D., *The Practice of Writing* (Penguin, 1997)
Martin, R., *Writing Historical Fiction* (A. & C. Black, 1988)
Stevenson, G., *How to Make Money out of Writing* (Wildwood House, 1989)
Taylor, L., *The Writing Business* (Severn House, 1985)
Wells, G., *The Successful Writer's Handbook* (Papermac, 1990)

INDEX